W9-DJO-985

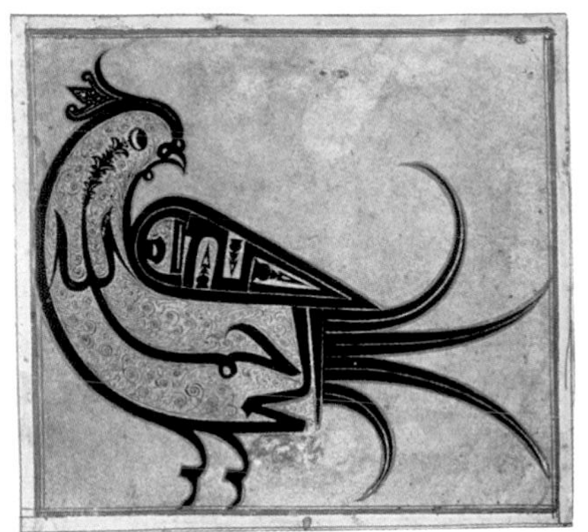

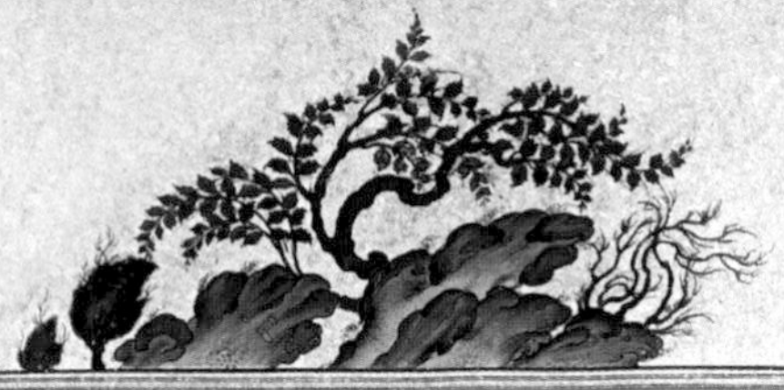

پشته چولی بکردار سام / بدیدش که می گشت گرد کنام
ره برشدن جست و کی بود راه / دد و دام را بر جهان جایگاه
بپوزش بر تو پسر افکنده ام / ز بر تپش تو جانرا پراکنده ام
گر این کودک از پاک پشت منست / نه از تخم بدگوهر اهرمنست
بدانست کو دادگر داور است / توانا و بر برتران برتر است
همی گفت کای برتر از جایگاه / ز روشن کان و ز خورشید و ماه
ازین برشدن بنده را دستگیر / مر این پر گنه را تو کن دلپذیر 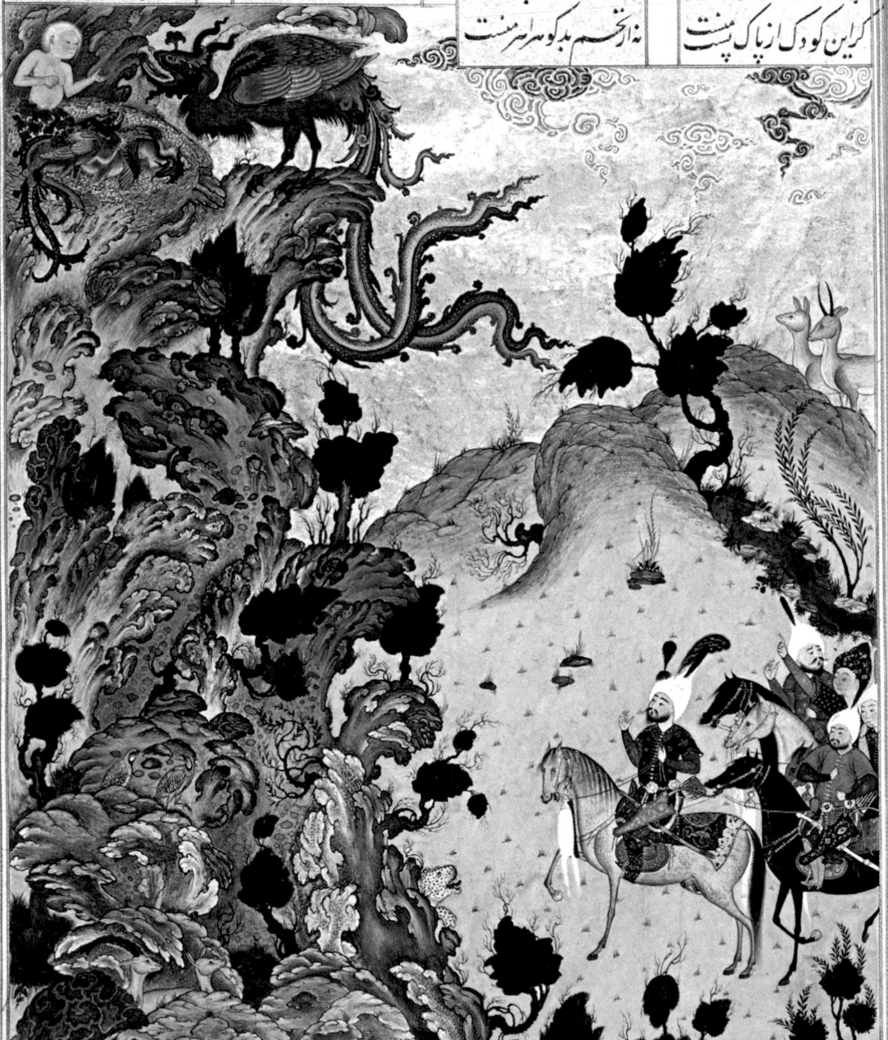
برحمت برافراز این بنده را / بمن باز ده پور افکنده را
چو با داور این راز ناگفته شد / ستایش همانا که پذرفته شد

Islamic Art

ANNETTE HAGEDORN
NORBERT WOLF (ED.)

TASCHEN
HONG KONG KÖLN LONDON LOS ANGELES MADRID PARIS TOKYO

خادم قد علته كبرة وعرته عبرة وقال يا قوم لا توسعونا سبًّا ولا توجعونا

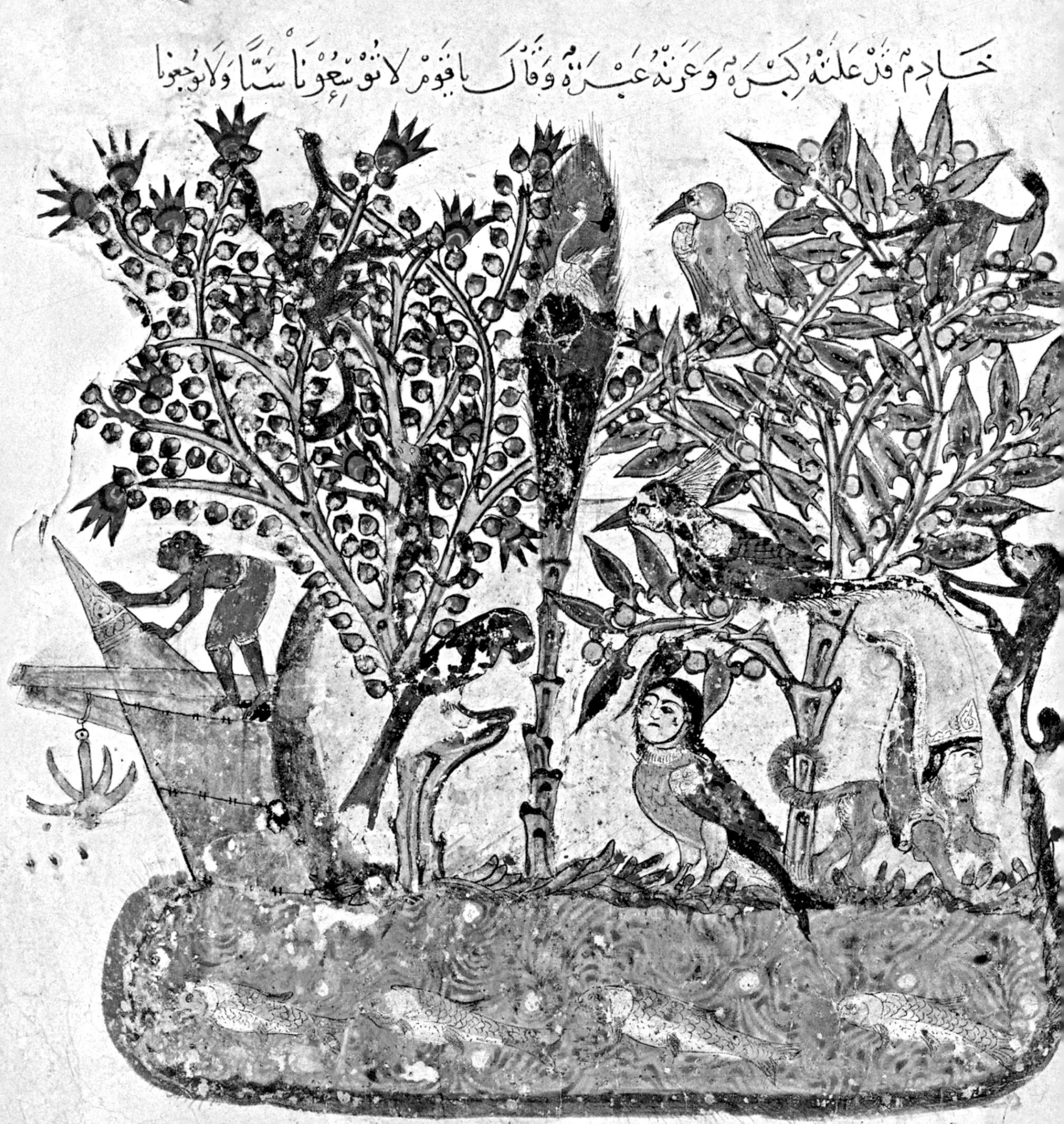

عتبا فانا لفي حزن شامل وشغل عن الحديث شاغل فقال له ابو زيد نفّس خناقاً ولمّ البثّ.

contents

Art of the Islamic world

European travelers, including artists and scholars, have been excited by Islamic art ever since the Middle Ages. Crusaders returned home with beautiful objects and many collections were started – even though the message communicated in such treasured images was often not understood. The influences exerted by this art are apparent – with interruptions – up to the present day. In 1907 painter Wassily Kandinsky (1866–1944) visited Berlin's Kaiser Friedrich Museum with its great Islamic collection and wrote home to St. Petersburg about the Persian paintings there: "It seemed unbelievable that this could have been created by human hands. Standing before it, I felt this had come into being of its own accord, as if it had come down from heaven like a revelation".

Artists continue to be inspired by the Islamic world. They are still fascinated by the light in Morocco and Tunisia, and by the geometry of huge, empty areas of sand in the Sahara. They also admire collections of Islamic art, absorbed by this art's capacity for abstraction. Paul Klee (1879–1940), Louis Moilliet (1880–1962), and August Macke (1887–1914) undertook their celebrated journey to Tunisia in 1914 for similar reasons.

Conversely, many parts of the Islamic world have absorbed artistic influences from Europe. That is especially true of Persia and India, which came into closer contact from the 16th century. From at least the time of its expansion into Europe the Ottoman Empire cultivated active political and cultural relations with the West, even to an excessive degree in the 17th and 18th centuries. These relations led to an artistic dialogue still to be observed in painting from the contemporary Islamic world.

Today Islam is in many cases publicly misrepresented, so the way in which Islamic art and culture are perceived in the Western world, the way in which Islamic art is received and comprehended, is becoming increasingly volatile.

Unlike "Christian" or "Buddhist" ways of comprehending art, "Islamic art" does not only entail objects directly linked with religion. This designation refers in general terms to the art which has been produced since the 7th century in regions where the Islamic faith prevails. However, it should not be forgotten that the Islamic world includes many countries – from Morocco to China and Indonesia – with cultural traditions of their own. So these works of art can be presented in accordance with their place of origin and ordered in terms of their date of creation under different Islamic dynasties. On the other hand, the unity of the Islamic world must be emphasized in order to show what is particularly "Islamic" about this art. In the pages that follow, attention

c. 570 — Birth of the Prophet Muhammad at Mecca

622 — Muhammad's flight from Mecca to Medina; start of the Islamic calendar

632 — Death of Muhammad in Medina

633–640 — Muslim conquest of Syria, Palestine, and today's Iraq

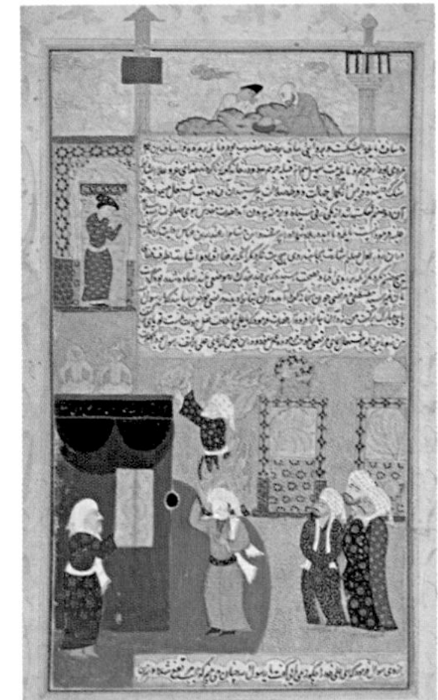

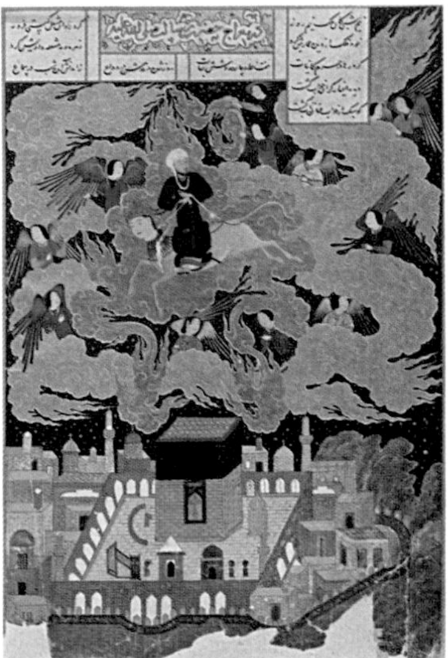

1. UNKNOWN ARTIST

The Prophet Muhammad Removes Idols from the Kaaba
Iran (Shiraz), 1585–1595 (Safavid), miniature from *Rawdat al-Safa* ("Garden of Purity") by Mir Khwand (d. 1498 in Herat), tempera on paper, colors, gold in the frame-painting, 29.3 x 17 cm
Berlin, Staatliche Museen zu Berlin – Preussischer Kulturbesitz, Museum of Islamic Art

2. ABD AL-RAZZAQ

Muhammad's Heavenly Journey Above the Kaaba
Afghanistan (Herat), 1494/1495, text from Nizami's *Khamsa* ("Five Stories"), opaque watercolors, gold on paper, 21 x 14 cm
London, The British Library

will also be devoted to interrelationships and the way in which Muslim countries influenced one another, so as to explain the development of Islamic art from its beginnings up to modern times. From the start this art inclined towards abstraction and stylization. Unlike the Christian West this style changed only slowly over the course of time since the search for new forms was thought less important than orientation towards older models.

calligraphy and illumination

The art form of calligraphy can perhaps be seen as Islamic culture's most important achievement. It is easy to understand that the Qur'an, as Muslims' Holy Book, had to be made particularly beautiful. Visual representation was not permitted here, so Arabic script became the most important element. Islamic faith and culture were disseminated in many parts of the world in conjunction with the Qur'an – and in close association with calligraphy – and thus established the foundation for a shared view of the world and a shared culture for all Muslims. So for the Islamic world the written word and the book are of the greatest cultural and artistic importance. The activities of reading and writing are indivisibly linked with the practice of religion, so from the beginning the art of writing gave rise to exquisite beauty and was much venerated. Calligraphy and book-illumination came into existence as early as the 7th century, mainly emphasizing balanced distribution of letters and the structuring of individual signs. In addition manuscripts were embellished with ornamented bindings utilizing color and gold. Calligraphy has always been highly prized in Islamic culture. Acquiring calligraphic expertise often took years and was even viewed as a princely virtue. That is why large libraries came into existence at courts, accompanied by calligraphy workshops employing artists from many countries. Until the 9th or 10th century calligraphers themselves also decorated manuscripts, but later there was increasing specialization between different activities with writers, calligraphers, painters of ornamentation, experts in gilding, and bookbinders.

In the Islamic world there were no definitions of aesthetic ideals as had existed in Europe since the Renaissance. The characteristics of Islamic aesthetics must therefore be deduced from the ways in which artists and men of letters responded to ancient guidelines and models. Right from the start such long-established ideas about beauty, harmony, and proportion were taken over in Islamic culture with balance and

651 — Start of Muslim rule in Iran **c. 657 — Battle of Siffin (near Raqqa in today's Syria) between supporters of Ali and of Mu'awiya; death of Ali in 661; since that time there have been Sunnis, Shiites, and Shariadites**

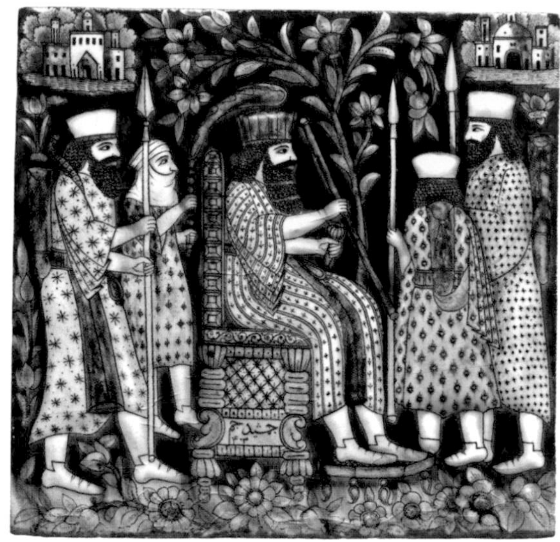

3

"The world assembled round his throne in wonder. At this resplendet fortune, while on him The people scattert jewels, and bestowed upon the day the name of New Year's Day, The first of Farwardin and for the year, … And ever since that time that glorious day Remaineth the memorial of shah Jamshid."

Firdawsi, Shahnama ("Book of Kings"), 1020

consonance appreciated as a supreme virtue in both poetry and the visual arts. Islamic artists and theorists tirelessly stressed that harmony was the crucial foundation for artistic beauty. The depiction of order and balance – as in the geometry of stellar ornamentation – was seen as a way of giving expression to the nature of God. Geometric patterns should thus not be understood merely as something purely decorative but also as an expression of philosophical concepts intended to manifest the beauty of God.

Calligraphic ornamentation of Qur'an manuscripts has existed since the 8th and 9th centuries whereas no representational book-painting from this period survives. Nevertheless everything indicates that there were also illustrated manuscripts at that time since abstract depictions of animals and human beings were part of the repertoire of ceramics decoration in Egypt and a little later in Persia. The first surviving book-paintings date from the early 11th century when a start was made on Arabic translations of scientific texts written in Greek and Syrian. Two such manuscripts were completed as early as 1010: *De materia medica* ("The Plant Book of Dioscorides") from the first century AD and the *Kitab Suwar al-Kawakib al-Thabita* ("Book of the Fixed Stars") by Abd al-Rahman ibn Umar al-Sufi (903–986). These are adorned with simple pen-and-ink drawings employing only a few emphases in color. Manuscripts illustrated throughout in color are only known from the 13th century (ill. p. 12, left, and ill. p. 20).

Soon such literary texts as the *Maqamat* ("Assemblies") by al-Hariri (1053–1122) were also illustrated, and these were popular both at royal courts and among rich merchants. Stylistically these paintings were very similar to Christian manuscripts of the same period, demonstrating the closeness of cultural exchange between the various religious and ethnic groups in the Eastern Mediterranean (ills p. 36, 37).

Muhammad and the Beginnings of Islamic Art

The Prophet Muhammad was born around 570 in the Arabian city of Mecca. His parents died when he was still young, so he was brought up first by his grandfather and then by an uncle. At 25 he married Khadijah bint Khuwaylid, a merchant's widow, and from that time traveled through the countries of Northern Arabia as a trader. There he came into contact with Jews, Christians, and Hanifiyya ("hanif" is the word used in the Qur'an for men and women who led the way in acceptance of monotheism). The Hanifiyya wanted to go beyond

691 — Completion of the Dome of the Rock in Jerusalem
710 — Muslim army reaches the Indus
706–715 — Construction of the Great Mosque in Damascus
711 — Muslim troops in Spain

3. ANONYMOUS

King Jamshid
Iran (Tehran), late 19th century (Qajaran), tile, earthenware, painted blue, turquoise, brown, and pink beneath the transparent glaze. Depicted is the mythological Iranian King Jamshid (the fourth Regent in Firdawsi's *Shahnama*), here dressed as an Achaemenid ruler with armed followers and a veiled servant, height 20.8 cm
London, The British Museum

4. ANONYMOUS

Depiction of a Stylized Mosque
Iran (probably Kashan), early 14th century, tile, quartz-chip ceramics, with verses from the Qur'an painted (partly in golden-brown luster) on the matt-white glaze. Blue glaze for the Qur'an verses at the periphery, the capitals, and the mosque lamps hanging from the arch, height 62 cm
London, Victoria and Albert Museum

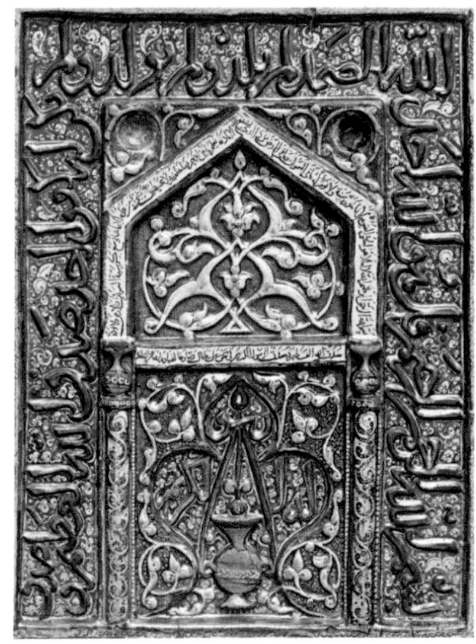

4

the traditional polytheism of Arab religions and believed in only one God. These encounters influenced Muhammad, who at that time had already started to call in question Mecca's preoccupation with material wealth. He thus withdrew from society to meditate on Mount Hira, close to Mecca. Here, in 610, the Archangel Gabriel appeared to Muhammad, revealing the Words of Allah – later recorded in the Qur'an. Initially Muhammad only spoke to his wife about this experience, but from the age of 40 he began to preach in public, criticizing the immorality of life in Mecca. To start with, the city's inhabitants did not take his sermons seriously, but that turned to violent rejection once Muhammad's preaching was regarded as endangering economic and religious order. After the death of his highly supportive wife and his uncle, the Prophet decided to move to Yathrib (later Medina). The date of his leaving Mecca in September 622, known as the *Hijra*, marks the beginning of the Islamic calendar. The number of Mohammad's followers constantly increased in the 620s and he gained victories over the Mecca merchant clans and various Jewish groups.

According to Muslim tradition, the Prophet died on 8 June 632. Scenes from his life have only been painted since the 15th century (ill. p. 7) with Muhammad's face often veiled in these depictions. In this miniature his son-in-law Ali, standing on the Prophet's shoulders, is shown removing the golden idols from the Kaaba (Arabic *ka'bah,* cube), Islam's epicenter at Mecca. This is viewed as symbolizing a fresh start initiated by Islam. The Kaaba itself is covered with a black cloth. Illustration 2 on p. 7 shows Mecca's Grand Mosque with the Kaaba in its courtyard. The architectural structure of this mosque – with a prayer hall equally divided into many transepts and a courtyard in front – was modeled on the Prophet's dwelling. This structure quickly established itself throughout the Islamic world – and from the 13th century was depicted in Mesopotamian book illumination and later in other art-forms (ill. p. 9). A mosque also includes one or several minarets and a fountain. Inside the prayer area is the *mihrab*, a niche pointing towards Mecca as orientation for prayer (*qibla)*, and the *minbar* (a pulpit; ill. p. 40). Among the many artistically adorned artifacts furnishing mosques are prayer mats (ill. p. 87), lecterns (in Turkish a *rahle*; detail: ill. p. 12 left), Qur'anic inscriptions (ills p. 29, 41), lamps (detail: ill. p. 9), and candelabra for providing light. Depictions of human beings are not found in mosques since Islam forbids this in places of religious observance.

732 — Charles "the Hammer" defeats the Muslims near Poitiers

751 — Start of the manufacture of paper in the Arab world

786–809 — Reign of Abbasid Caliph Harun al-Rashid in Spain

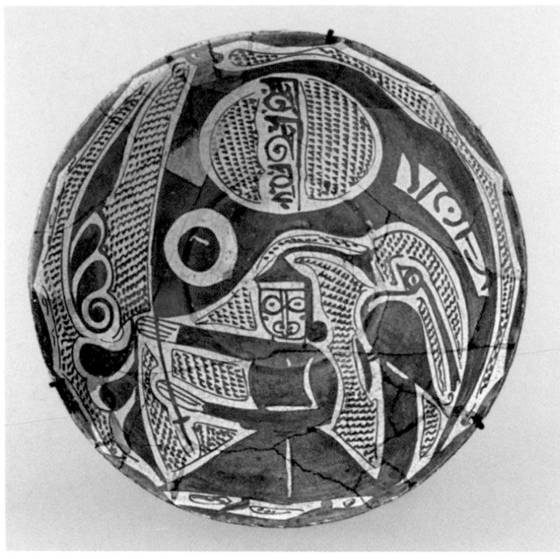

5

5. BOWL
Iraq, 10th century (Abbasid), ceramic with luster-painting, diameter 31.8 cm
Paris, Musée du Louvre

6. BEAKER
Iran (Kashan), late 12th century, earthenware with Minai glaze, illustrating a scene from the *Shahnama* ("Book of Kings") by Firdawsi (940/941–1020), the Persian poet. This tells the story of Bizhan and Manizha, height 11.2 cm
Washington, DC, Freer Gallery of Art

Art under the Umayyads and Abbasids

During the 8th century Islam spread quickly so that the entire region from Spain to Central Asia followed the new religion. Syria became the most important artistic center during this period. Here older traditions survived particularly well since Late Antiquity's most significant strands of culture came together in this area. In the North was the Byzantine Empire with its highly developed Christian culture where much had been preserved of Greco-Roman art. A rich artistic legacy also existed in countries to the East (Iraq and Persia) where a new high culture developed in the centuries immediately before Islamic conquest under the Sassanids (224–651). In addition, during Classical Antiquity, the region to the South (Egypt and North Africa) was a highly developed center of culture with its own traditions, which continued in existence in a changed form under Islamic rule.

The Umayyads (661–750) ruled from Damascus as successors to the first four Caliphs chosen from Muhammad's family circle. In 696/697 they reformed the currency and introduced Arabic as the official language, which facilitated trade and led to mounting prosperity in the Islamic world.

Eclecticism (i.e. taking up different models and making them into a new style: ills. p. 17, 31) was a typical characteristic of Umayyad art. That was possible because in the 7th and 8th centuries many older buildings still existed and could be studied. In addition, the Umayyads brought artists and craftsmen from many different areas to the Eastern Mediterranean. In Syria and Jordan the Caliphs had several palaces constructed to serve princely prestige and pleasure. In their fortress-like architecture these buildings were reminiscent of Roman frontier forts, and their interior decoration was based on Late Roman and Persian models. Rooms were often embellished with frescoes or with large stucco sculptures, sometimes including almost naked female figures (ill. p. 16). The most important early Islamic religious buildings, such as the Dome of the Rock in Jerusalem (691) and the Great Mosque in Damascus (705–715), were also built under the Umayyads. Their highly symbolic non-figurative ornamentation was an important influence on the development of a specifically Islamic art.

Very few examples of applied art from the Early Islamic period have survived. The textiles demonstrate great stylistic and technical affinities with Egyptian materials. Glass and works in metal are close to Byzantine and Sassanid products, and creations in ivory were influenced

969 — Fatimid foundation of the city of Cairo
1061 — Normans drive Muslims out of Sicily
1067 — Plundering of the Fatimid Palace in Cairo; its treasures end up all across the Islamic world and in Europe

"No room was left for further parleying.
Forth from beneath the shadow of the cypress
Bizhan proceeded hastily afoot
Toward Manizha's tent and entered it,
In favour like a stately cypress tree,
Girt with a golden girdle round his loins."

Firdawsi, Shahnama ("Book of Kings"), 1020

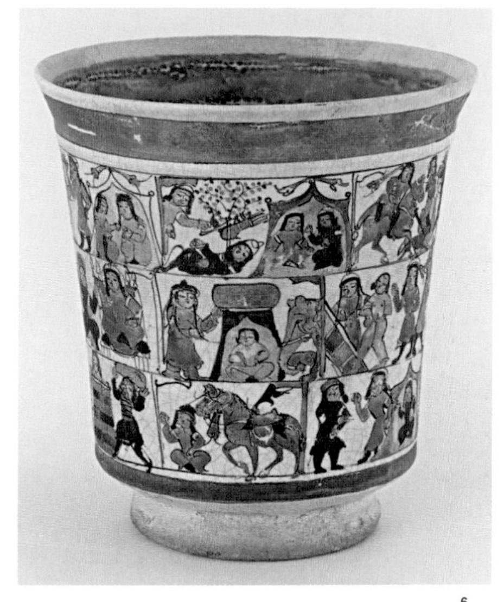

6

by Classical Antiquity. Later objects made of metal were frequently melted down so that very few still exist today. One that did survive is a large bronze *aquamanile* ("water jug") with inlays of silver and copper, made in 796/797 by an artist named Suleiman (ill. p. 14 right). Its bird-shape and embellishment with a *Kufic* inscription (ancient rectilinear script) and stylized feathers clearly indicate links with Persian Sassanid art. As this piece shows, figurative depictions outside a religious context were by no means excluded in ornamentation of utilitarian objects and in architectural detail. Even people could be shown as in a piece of pottery (ill. p. 10) showing a standard-bearer with a peacock. However, these figures are highly stylized and do not cast any shadow so as to avoid seeming really alive – since religion forbade such depictions.

Another form of Early Islamic ornamentation is to be found on a 9th-century carved door (ill. p. 15 left), believed to come from Samarra which for a short time was the capital of the Abbasid Dynasty (749–1258). This demonstrates strictly geometrical division of space and structuring, as also employed in stucco ornamentation in the range of architecture.

The Art of Western Islamic Countries

In the 7th century Muslim armies conquered the whole of North Africa *(Ifriqiya)* as far as the Atlantic. From 711 most of Spain also came under their rule after Tariq ibn Ziyad (670–720) defeated the last Western Goth prince at Jerez de la Frontera. The country was initially ruled by the Caliphs' governors, but when the Abbasids seized power in the Eastern Mediterranean, Abd al-Rahman (756–788), the only survivor of the Umayyad Dynasty, fled to Spain and in the year 756 established the Emirate of Cordoba. In the centuries that followed Spain experienced a Golden Age when its rulers enabled Muslims, Christians, and Jews to live together peacefully. That gave rise to both economic prosperity and a vital exchange of knowledge and culture between the different religions. Under Abd al-Rahman III (912–961) many architectural masterpieces were built, with the royal city of Medina al-Zahra and Cordoba's enlarged mosque still famous down to the present day. The stucco ornamentation of buildings in Medina al-Zahra is based on stylized plant motifs from the Middle East, sometimes dating back to the pre-Islamic period. Craftsmen from Byzantium, Syria, and Egypt were summoned to imitate the ornamentation of Damascus' Great Mosque when its counterpart in Cordoba was extended. That

1095–1099 — First Crusade **1099 — Crusaders' conquest of Jerusalem**
1171–1260 — Saladin and his successors, the Ayyubids, rule Syria and Egypt

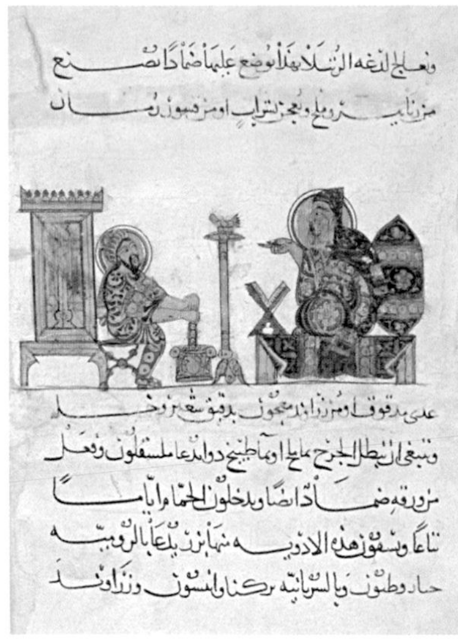

7

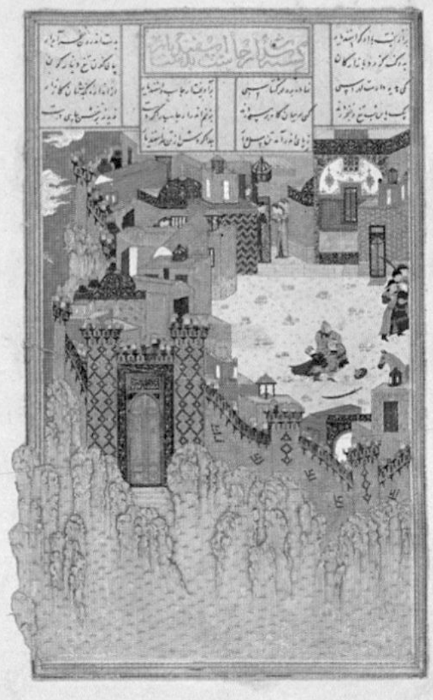

8

7. ABDALLAH IBN AL-FADL

Doctor and Assistant Prepare a Poultice
In: *Kitab al-Hashaish*, Iraq (Baghdad), 1224 (Abbasid), miniature from a translation of Dioscorides' *De materia medica* (1st century), 33.1 x 24.6 cm (detail)
Washington, DC, Freer Gallery of Art

8. UNKNOWN ARTIST

Arjasp Wrestled to Death by Isfandiar
Iran, c. 1444, opaque watercolors, ink, gold on paper, 34 x 22 cm
London, The Royal Asiatic Society

led to cultural links between diverse regions around the Mediterranean, influencing all aspects of the visual arts. Western Islamic pottery of the 10th-century, with both calligraphic designs and figurative themes, thus demonstrates great similarities with work from further East. Applied art (ills p. 44, 45) simultaneously took up forms from architectural decoration, adopting its underlying system of structuring surfaces with arabesques, surface ornamentation, and skillfully deployed inscriptions.

Around 1013 the Spanish Caliphate broke up into over two dozen autonomous little kingdoms. Shortly afterwards at least part of the country came under the rule of the Almoravids (1056–1147), a Berber Dynasty which came to power in North Africa in the 11th century. During this period there were lively artistic exchanges between Spain and the countries of North Africa. In 1070 the Almoravids founded the city of Marrakesh in today's Morocco, but they only reigned briefly in other cities such as Saragossa in Spain.

Morocco and Tunisia were greatly influenced by Spanish art. The Berbers were involved in extensive caravan trade with the Eastern Mediterranean, so textiles, ceramics, and glass from there reached Islamic countries in the West. However, one cannot speak of "Berber art" in the centers of the Almoravid kingdom at that time since urbane Egyptian and Syrian models also influenced native craftsmen through trade. In addition, architecture's stucco ornamentation of written friezes continued to have an impact on applied art.

A revival of autonomous Spanish art occurred during the 13th century. Here, too, Cordoba served as the country's intellectual center. However, this flourishing was of brief duration since in 1212 the Almohads (1130–1269), then in power, were defeated by the Christian Kings and had to leave Andalusia in 1225. Nevertheless, the Muslim population largely remained in the country and a final cultural blossoming occurred in those parts of Southern Spain still under Islamic rule. In Granada construction of the Alhambra, the royal castle of the Nasrids (1232–1492), began in 1238. Tiled and stuccoed walls were adorned in the Muslim tradition with plant and calligraphic motifs, and quickly seen as the epitome of well-conceived structural art.

The end of Moorish rule finally came in 1492 when the kingdom of Granada was conquered by Ferdinand of Aragon and Isabella of Castile, and Spain was once again completely allied with Christian Europe. However, even after Muslim rulers had left the country, the art and culture of the Iberian Peninsula were long indebted to the Islamic legacy and its sources. Here developed what is known as the *Mudejar*

1212 — Almohads defeated by Christian Kings near Navas de Tolosa
1258 — Mongol conquest of Baghdad
1281 — Mamluks under al-Malik al-Mansur Qalawun defend Hims (Syria) against the Mongols; end of the Mongol advance westwards

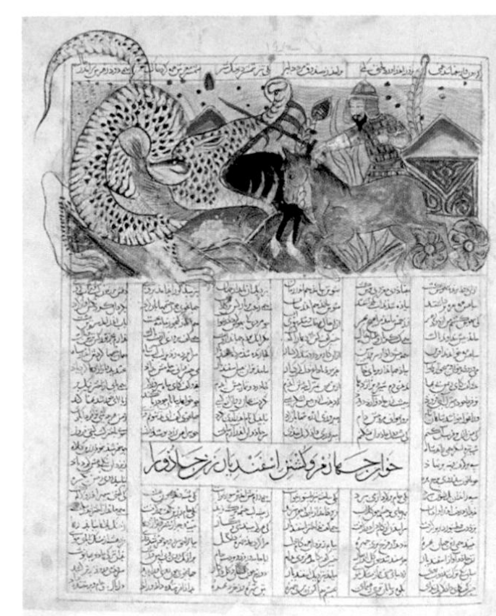

9

9. UNKNOWN ARTIST

Isfandiar's Battle with the Dragon
Iran (Shiraz), 1330 (Injuid dynasty), miniature from the *Shahnama* ("Book of Kings") by Firdawsi (940/941–1020), the Persian poet, 11 x 23 cm
Istanbul, Topkapi Palace Museum

style, characterized by an intermingling of Christian-European and Islamic-Eastern elements.

From the late 18th century Andalusia's geometrical ornamentation has exerted a considerable influence on European applied art. Architectural motifs and 14th and 15th century ceramics, carpets, and metalwork have left their mark on art and art theory in the North. Study of Moorish models even played an essential part in development of new principles of design in modern art by Owen Jones (1809–1874), William Morris (1834–1896), William de Morgan (1839–1917), and Karl Ernst Osthaus (1874–1921).

The Eastern Mediterranean in the High Middle Ages

The Fatimids

The Fatimid Dynasty ruled in Sicily, Tunisia, and elsewhere in North Africa before conquering Egypt in 969 and moving its palace to the newly established Cairo. From there the Fatimids pursued the conquest of Syria and Mesopotamia. The dynasty derived its descent and claim to dominance from the Prophet's daughter Fatima. As the first Islamic ruling dynasty the Fatimids upheld the Shia conviction that Muhammad's successors as Muslim leader had to come from the Prophet's family. Linked with that idea was the hope that the *Mahdi* would appear as a charismatic leader implementing just rule over all Muslims. Ultimately the Fatimids thereby attempted to establish a counter-caliphate to the Abbasid rulers in Baghdad, but they were only briefly successful.

The Fatimids supported the construction of roads and canals and promoted trade between India and the Mediterranean area, so business in their kingdom experienced an enormous boom. In Cairo a number of important mosques were built and (from 1087) strong city fortifications intended to provide protection against the Turkish Seljuks who had just captured Jerusalem. Their prosperity allowed the Fatimid rulers to cultivate an extremely luxurious lifestyle and to promote art. Nevertheless, there was a crisis between 1067 and 1069 when Caliph al-Mustansir (1036–1094) got into difficulty over payment of his Turkish soldiers and was forced to sell all his art treasures. In his *Kitab al-Hadaya wa al-Tuhaf* ("Book of Treasures and Precious Objects") historian al-Maqrizi (1364–1442) describes – on the basis of old sources – all the works sold on this occasion. According to that account the Fatimid rulers possessed valuable manuscripts, skillfully

1323 — Peace between Mongols and Mamluks

1357 — Ottomans arrive in Europe; conquest of the Gallipoli Peninsula by Suleyman Pasha

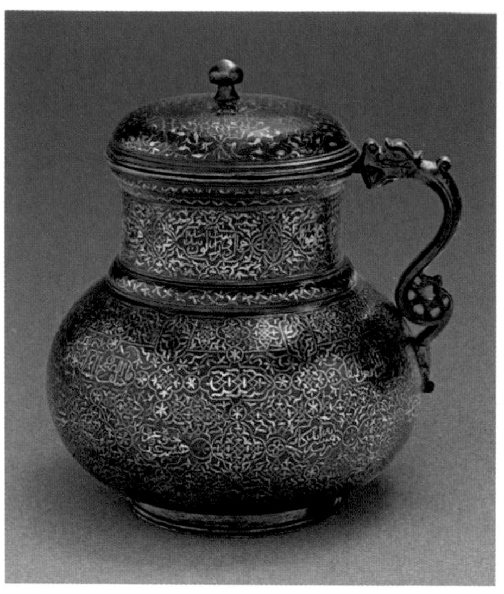

10

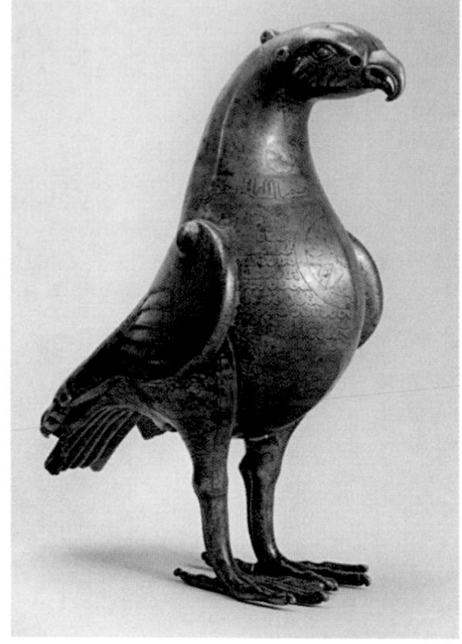

11

10. HUSAIN IBN MUBARAK-SHAH

Jug
Afghanistan (Herat), 1484–1485, brass with silver and gold inlays
Doha, Museum of Islamic Art, MW.471.2007

11. SULEIMAN

Aquamanile in the form of a Bird of Prey
Probably Iraq, 796/797, (Abbasid), bronze with silver and copper inlays. On the neck incomplete *Kufic* inscription invoking *Bismillah* (Allah), height 38 cm
St. Petersburg, Hermitage State Museum

carved ivory (ill. p. 15 right), precious textiles, and ceramics (ills p. 34, 35), and objects in metal. The few surviving pieces show that Fatimid art was highly developed and of great elegance and beauty, particularly in its depiction of human figures. The motifs followed many traditions, some of them extending back into antiquity. Their stylistic richness and refinement impressed even European Princes and was imitated, especially at the court of Sicily's Norman rulers.

Ayyubids, crusaders, and seljuks

After the death of al-Mustansir in 1094 unrest erupted. In the same year the First Crusade got under way. European armies conquered parts of Syria and Lebanon without encountering any great resistance. In 1099 Jerusalem fell and in 1104 Akkon. The Crusaders established fortresses and harbors, and began to settle the Levant. For two centuries that resulted in a fusion of the traditions of Eastern Islamic culture and European Christian art. When Saladin (1137–1193) seized power, Fatimid dominance finally came to an end and the rise of the Ayyubid Dynasty began. In 1183 Saladin conquered Aleppo, in 1186 Mosul, in 1187 Jerusalem, and in 1188 the Crusader states of Tripoli and Antioch. Only after his defeat in 1191 by Richard I of England (1189–1199) was a provisional balance of power established between Islamic and Christian rulers.

The age of the Crusades was an epoch of courtliness in both the Eastern Mediterranean and Western Europe. In the East urbane rulers possessed all kinds of art objects serving the staging of courtly culture. On many of these objects were inscriptions, either expressing good wishes for the owners or calling on those who commissioned them to act virtuously, justly, compassionately, and nobly. These royal courts were not just acting as patrons of art; works of art simultaneously demonstrated their power. Above all, prestigious public buildings, minting money, and the staging of rulers' public appearances so obviously served self-presentation that one can speak here of political art. Most of the surviving paintings from this period came into existence in Mesopotamia, the Land of Two Rivers. This was not a politically unified area. After Alp Arsan's (1063–1072) victory over Byzantium at Manzikert (today Malazgirt) in 1071, Turkish troops pushed forward into Asia Minor. In 1077 the Anatolian Rum-Seljuk Dynasty was founded and the Turkish take-over of the region got under way. In the area between today's Southern Turkey and Baghdad many small principalities came into existence and their rulers were often great art-

1370–1506 — Timurid rule of the area around the city of Bukhara (Transoxania) and in Iran with Samarkand as capital
1398–1399 — Tamerlane conquers India and plunders Delhi; up to 1401 conquest of Syria and plundering of Damascus

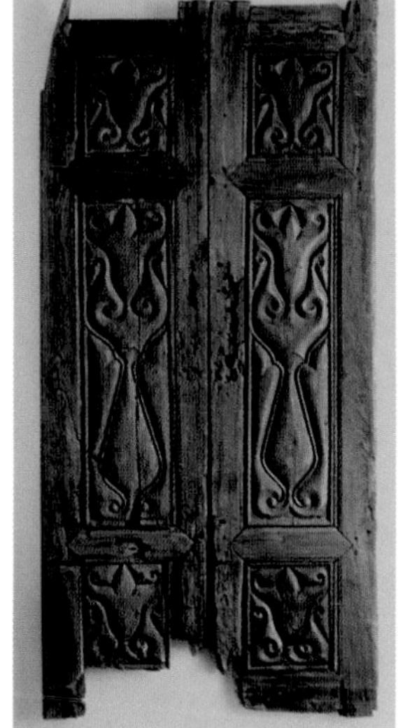

12

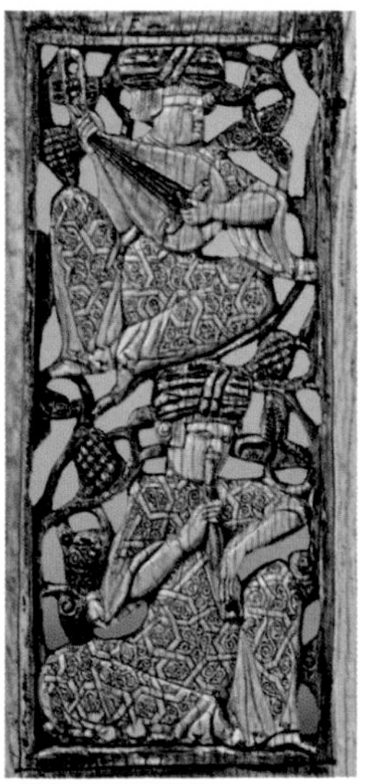

13

12. WOODEN DOOR (FRAGMENT)
Probably Iraq (Samarra), 9th century (Abbasid), carved wood, 222.9 x 106.7 cm
New York, NY, The Metropolitan Museum of Art

13. IVORY CARVING WITH MUSICIANS (DETAIL)
Egypt, 11th century (Fatimid), ivory, 13 x 18 cm
Florence, Museo Nationale del Bargello

lovers, implemented active building programs, and had their own court workshops. Among these small states were Diyarbakir, Diyar Mudar, and Diyar Rabi'a, containing such important cities as Mardin, Mosul, Sinjar, and Raqqa. In addition Baghdad was the capital of the Greater Seljuk Empire.

Mosul offers a characteristic example of the splendor of those principalities. Under Badr al-Din Lulu (*Atabeg*/Governor 1210–1234; Ruler 1234–1259) an important school for metalwork was developed with valuable art objects made of brass with inlays of silver and gold. Many pieces make a great show of courtly motifs with scenes around the throne or depictions of the monarch as horseman or huntsman, or as participant in festivities with musicians and women dancers. However, there also exist scenes based on the *Shahnama*, the Persian "Book of Kings", by Firdawsi (940/941–1020). The style and rich iconographic repertoire of these much-admired works even influenced painting. A little later such pieces were also produced in Cairo, Damascus, and Aleppo, and – after the Mongols captured Mosul – in Iran, too.

The Art of the Mamluks

After the crusaders had been driven out of the Middle East, the Mamluks began their rise to power (after 1250). They were originally Turkish bodyguards to the Ayyubid rulers of Egypt and Syria (the Arabic word *mamluk* means "somebody's property"). These slaves had been an important source of support for the Ayyubids' military system and this paved the way for their own access to power. In 1260 the Mamluks under Baibars (1260–1277) defeated the Mongols who had advanced westwards, compelling them to abandon Damascus and Aleppo. In 1280 Qalawun (1280–1290) came to power. He launched a ruthless campaign against Christian strongholds in the Eastern Mediterranean, and all the crusader states quickly succumbed.

The most important artistic period under the Mamluk Princes was during the regency of Sultan Hasan ibn Muhammad Nasir al-Din (1347–1351, and 1354–1361; ills p. 39, 40, 41, 43). His court workshops in Cairo and Damascus did not only produce ornamented manuscripts; they also designed and manufactured art objects in a wide range of materials (textiles, carpets, metal, glass, wood, and ivory). After 1330 religious dictates excluded figurative depictions in applied art, which led to a great flourishing of decorative calligraphy. As

1453 — Constantinople/Istanbul captured by the Ottomans
1520–1566 — Suleyman "the Magnificent" as Ottoman Sultan
1492 — Christians recapture Granada. Columbus discovers America
c. 1525–1535 — Most important "Shahnama" ("Book of Kings")

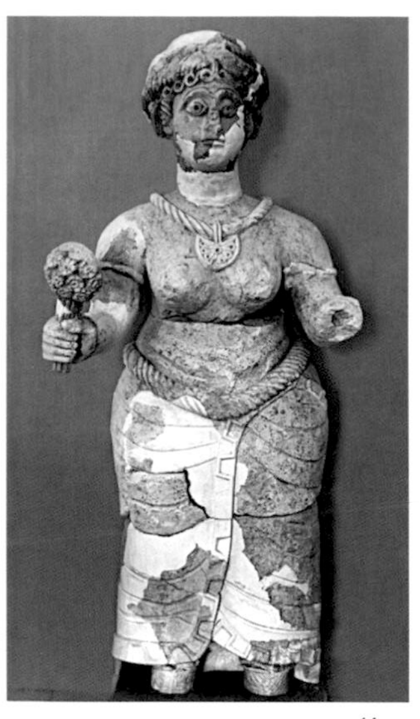

14

14. SCULPTURE OF A SCANTILY CLOTHED WOMAN
Khirbat al-Mafjar castle near Jericho, 724–743
Jerusalem, Rockefeller Museum

already in the 13th century, urban craftsmen had their own workshops at city markets. They both fulfilled commissions for the merchant class and court circles in their own country and also produced goods to be exported to Europe. Objects decorated with Arab calligraphy were highly sought in Italy and north of the Alps. This style was much admired, and what were seen as mysterious inscriptions adopted as a decorative element in European art.

In the 19th century there was renewed interest in Mamluk art. In Egypt, Syria, and Europe this was seen as being exemplary and worthy of imitation. Many Europeans traveled to Cairo to buy Mamluk artifacts and Egyptian craftsmen produced replicas and imitations to satisfy this demand. The architecture of that time also recalled styles from the 13th and 14th centuries. Such prestigious buildings as the al-Gezira palace constructed for the Ottoman Khedives ruling in Egypt (1869, to mark the opening of the Suez Canal), the Islamic Museum (1903), and the el-Rifai Museum (1912) were built in a renewed Mamluk style.

Persian Art from the Start of Mongol Rule

The Il-Khans (Ilkhanids)

The history of Persia in the 13th century was shaped by the advance of Mongol armies under Genghis Khan (1206–1227) and his successors. After Hulagu (1256–1265) had conquered Iran, Mesopotamia, and Syria there came into being the state of the Il-Khans (i.e. subordinate or peaceable Khans) as the most westerly Mongol realm, roughly comprising today's Iraq and Iran.

Mongol rulers discovered for their art the history and tradition of countries they had overrun. Important schools of book-illustration, taking up Persian models, came into existence at Isfahan and Tabriz. The Il-Khan (Ilkhanid) kingdom's close political and economic relations with East Asia resulted in incorporation of Chinese and Central Asian elements, and the pronounced stylization, which had predominated in works from the Baghdad school of painting, was now linked with the more lively Chinese style (ill. p. 52). In Tabriz, Abu Said's (1317–1335) *Vizier* ("Minister") Rashid al-Din (1247–1318) established a district where artists, scholars, and craftsmen lived and worked.

produced at Tabriz for Shah Tahmasp **1526 — Babur founds the Mogul Empire** **1529 — First Ottoman siege of Vienna**
1534 — Ottomans conquer Baghdad **1535 — Death of Bihzad, Persian painter**

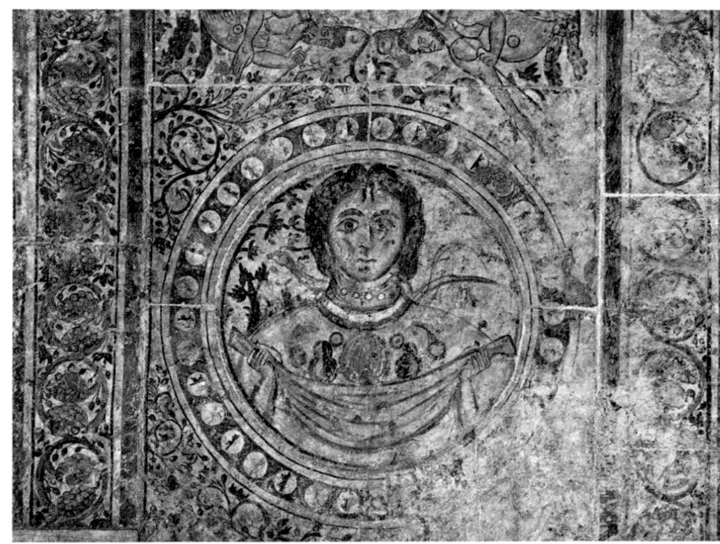
15

15. ANONYMOUS PAINTER OF MURALS

The Goddess Gaia among Vines
Syria, c. 724–727, fresco (detail), overall dimensions 10.87 x 4.45 m, from the south-eastern stairwell of the Qasr al-Hair al-Gharbi ("Western Residence") Umayyad palace in Syria, about 60 km west of Palmyra
Damascus, National Museum

Rashid al-Din also initiated the writing of a *Jami al-Tawarikh* ("Chronicle of the World") intended to further the new Mongolian-Iranian upper class' historical awareness (ill. p. 49).

The intention was to revive the idea of a Greater Iranian State, as is mainly demonstrated by the fact that an entire series of illustrated manuscripts of the Persian *Shahnama* ("Book of Kings") was now produced (ill. p. 13). This epic, written by Firdawsi (940/941–1020), can be interpreted as a work of Iranian history but also as a "Reflection of Exemplary Princely Behavior". The most important 14th-century *Shahnama* manuscript (ills p. 18, 59) was probably created for Abu Said at Tabriz in 1335/1336. Its particularly splendid miniatures are frequently highly dramatic in their presentation of landscapes, indicating a link with Persian literature and atmospheric descriptions of nature. Other *Shahnama* manuscripts were produced between 1330 and 1353 at the court of the Injuid Dynasty ruling in Shiraz (ill. p. 57). Their style makes clear the convergence of influences from Mesopotamia and East Asia.

Only at the end of the 14th century are the first signs of a new autonomy and greater stylistic unity to be seen in the painting of Greater Iran. An early example of this development is provided by a miniature from Baghdad, painted in 1396 by Ustad Junayd for a *Diwan* ("Collection of poems") manuscript (ill. p. 19).

Tamerlane and His Successors

The Il-Khan kingdom split into small regional states from 1335, but at the end of the 14th century Timur-i Lang (Tamerlane, 1370–1405) succeeded in once again establishing a Mongolian Empire. From 1380 onwards he subdued the Eastern countries, triumphantly penetrated as far as Delhi in 1398/1399, and at the start of the 15th century conquered Georgia, Anatolia, Syria, and Iraq.

Plundered works of art and artists from subjugated countries were carried off to Tamerlane's capital Samarkand. The architecture and art which originated there mainly served representation of the Prince's power. Tamerlane presented himself as an urbane ruler and patron of the arts. His successors also promoted the arts even though they were only local rulers. Mention should be made here of Tamerlane's son Shah Rukh (1405–1447) at whose court in Herat one of the most important Persian painting schools came into existence, and Shah Rukh's son Baisunghur Mirza (1420–1433) for whom the most talented artists and calligraphers worked.

Arts and crafts in many materials were produced in the court workshops, for instance a brass pot with silver and gold inlays (ill. p. 14 left), made by Husain ibn Mubarak-Shah in 1484. The floral

1550–1557 — Construction of the Suleymaniye Mosque in Istanbul **1571 — Sea battle of Lepanto (northern entrance to the Corinthian Gulf); beginning of the end of Ottoman dominance in the Mediterranean**

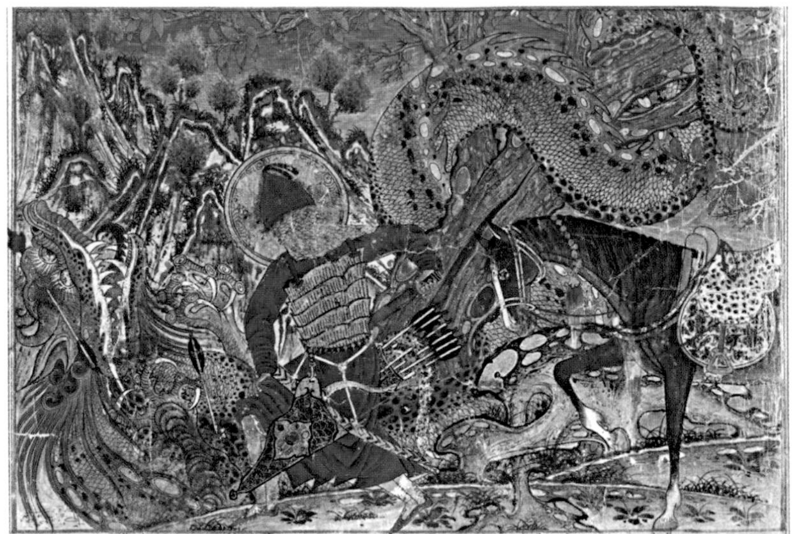

16

16. UNKNOWN ARTIST

Bahram Gur Kills a Dragon
Iran (possibly Tabriz), 1335/1336, ink, opaque watercolors, gold on paper, miniature 20 x 29 cm, entire page 45.5 x 34.2 cm
Cleveland, OH, The Cleveland Museum of Art

17. JUNAYD (PUPIL OF SHAMS)

Princess Humayun Sees Humay at the Gate of her Castle
Iraq (Baghdad), 1396 (Jalayirid), miniature from a manuscript of three poems by Khwaju Kirmani (b. 1280/1281), copyist: Mir Ali ibn Ilyas from Tabriz, 38.1 x 24.7 cm
London, The British Library

and calligraphic ornamentation, accompanied by a text in Arabic and Persian by the Persian poet Kulliyat-I Qasim (d. c. 1433), testifies to the court's great interest in calligraphy and poetry. The techniques of drawing were also taught in the workshops of Tabriz, Herat, and Samarkand, and there soon developed a unified style, followed by more or less all the artists of the 15th century. This Timurid "imperial style" is demonstrated in a manuscript from the *Kalila wa Dimna* collection of stories (ill. p. 24 right), showing a prince and his court in an idyllic garden. All these personages are depicted very naturally but not completely realistically; their faces are also characterized highly individually. This scene reflects the richness and harmony of life at cultured courts.

However, a miniature from a *Shahnama* manuscript dated 1444 (ill. p. 12 right) showing Arjasp and Isfandiar wrestling, demonstrates that intractable struggle could also be taken as a theme in book-illustration. Particularly impressive in this scene is the depiction of the castle, its towers adorned with tiles, and of the great diversity in other decorative aspects of the building, according with surviving Timurid architecture.

How well trained Timurid artists were in representing architecture also becomes apparent in the drawing of a city (ill. p. 20) whose compressed heterogeneity is comparable with the castle in the miniature – even though the lack of color and the simpler gradation of depth make the former seem less rich.

Bihzad the Painter

Persian painting reached a peak around 1500 at Herat where Sultan Husain Baiqara (1469–1506) and his Grand Vizier Mir Ali Shir Nawa'i (1441–1501) were great patrons of the arts. Bihzad was born there around 1450/1460 and became Persia's most famous painter. He probably stayed in his birthplace until 1510 and then moved to Tabriz where he worked until his death (between 1533 and 1537) at the court of Safavid rulers Shah Ismail (1501–1524) and Shah Tahmasp I (1524–1576), most likely as head of the court workshop (after 1522).

The young Bihzad was taught by various esteemed painters in Tabriz and later worked with such important artists as Aqa Mirak (d. before 1576; ill. p. 75). Six of his many pupils are still known today by name. In his miniatures Bihzad did not develop any really new style but he added to the achievements of the Herat school. His highly composed pictures live from the diversity of powerful colors and successful combination of different tones. Compared with older paintings, the figures

1609–1614 — Moors driven out of Spain **1647 — Construction of the Taj Mahal at Agra (India)**
1718–1730 — In the Ottoman Empire "Tulip Era" under Sultan Ahmed III; opening up to Western cultural influences

"The sun at midday shone brilliantly through the green tracery of leaves: a medley of light and shade covered the ground like a wealth of gold an musk. Aroused by the play of light, the song birds scattered their melodious trills beneath the turqoise vault."

Jami, Yusuf and Zulaikha, 1483

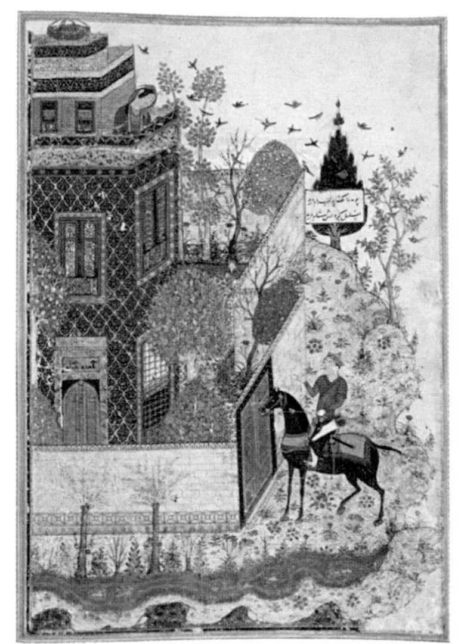

17

have gained in mobility and individuality, and bodily proportions are represented with great skill. Alongside traditional themes taken from literary texts, Bihzad also devoted himself to depiction of scenes close to daily reality. He thus painted workers constructing a mosque (1494/1495) or happenings in a public bath (ill. p. 71), demonstrating a gift for accurate observation. The buildings in his miniatures accord completely with architecture around 1500 and persons are dressed in the style of the times; warriors wear armor and carry weapons that are shown in detail; and objects in everyday use are also depicted as they really were. The artist's emphasis on decorative and harmonious landscapes plays a large part in the poetic and romantic mood of his pictures.

Bihzad's art was admired from the 16th to the 18th century and exerted considerable influence on the development of painting in very different areas of the Islamic world. Miniatures in an almost identical style were thus produced at the Bukharan court of the Shaybanids (1500–1599) and at Herat after the end of Timurid rule (1370–1506). The court workshops of the Mogul rulers in India (1526–1858) and the Persian Safavids (1501–1732) in Tabriz, Qazwin, and Isfahan were also shaped by the Bihzad School. Traces of his style are also recognizable in Ottoman art, since many Persian manuscripts reached Istanbul and directly influenced artists working there.

The safavids

The Turkmen dynasty of Safavids determined the history of Iran between 1501 and 1768. After driving out the last of the Mongols under Shah Ismail I (1501–1524), they first established their palace in Tabriz, then at Qazwin, and finally in Isfahan. Splendid works of art were produced in their court workshops: silver and gold vessels studded with jewels, valuable riding accoutrements, and precious, richly illustrated manuscripts. The tasks of court artists also included the preparation of designs for carpets and large tiled areas (ill. p. 77).

A degree of artistic decline is apparent in mid-16th-century Qazwin, where religious considerations led Shah Tahmasp I (1524–1576) to lose interest in book illustration and in 1555 even close down his *Kitabhane* ("Book House", or writing workshop). Many of the artists dismissed then worked for other members of the ruler's family. Calligrapher and painter Shah Mahmud al-Nishapuri (1486–1565) thus went to the workshop of Ibrahim Mirza (1540–1577) in Mashad, where in 1565 he and other artists created miniatures for a manuscript of Jami's (1414–1492) *Haft Aurang* ("Seven Thrones").

1726 — Introduction of book printing

1761 — Treaty of Friendship between the Ottoman Empire and Prussia

1779 — Foundation of the Qajar Dynasty in Iran under Agha Muhammad with Iran as capital

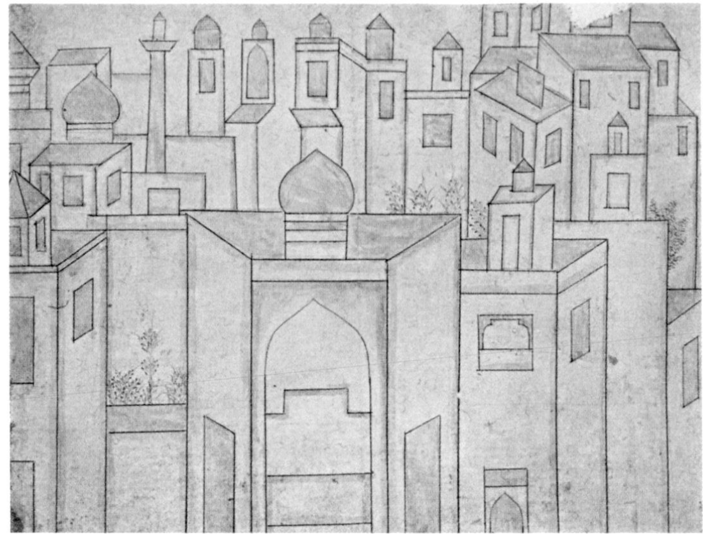

18

> **"Houses tell stories. Nothing tells better stories than what people have built."**
>
> Abu Ja'far al-Idrisi (1173–1251)

The Safavids cultivated contacts with Europe as well as relations with China. With support from England Shah Abbas I (1588–1629) reformed the Persian military and with his new army was able to defeat the Ottomans in 1603 and re-conquer areas around Tabriz and large parts of Iraq including Baghdad. After, Shah Abbas also succeeded in driving the Uzbeks out of the region around Samarkand and Herat, the Safavid Empire was at its height both politically and culturally. Once again, art and architecture enjoyed patronage, and an important art school came into existence at Isfahan.

One of the main painters in Shah Abbas I's court workshop was Aqa Riza (d. 1635). Two of his works – *Day-Dreaming Youths Resting in a Garden*, and *Young Man Day-Dreaming* (ill. p. 21 left) – are characteristic of the style of that period and at the same time represent Safavid culture's ideal existence. Other artists preferred to depict resplendent court ceremonies such as Abbas II's (1642–1666) reception for the Indian ambassador (ill. p. 22). The richness of clothing and weapons deployed on such occasions is apparent here; and so, too, is the lavish furnishing of rooms with valuable carpets and porcelain. How differently Mu'in Musavvir (active 1638–1697) worked when producing a portrait becomes clear when this luxurious scene with its many figures is compared to his portrayal of court official Nawab Mirza Muhammad Baqir and his son (ill. p. 23). Musavvir's concentration on a single person and a particular ambiance is close to the poetic creations of Aqa Riza.

Art under India's Mogul Rulers

In the 8th century Muslim armies advanced into India by way of Afghanistan. However, lasting Islamic dominance only began with seizure of power by Mahmud of Ghur (1173–1206) and establishment of the Delhi Sultanate by Qutb al-Din Aybak (1206–1210). When disputes broke out in the 16th century between rival noble families, one of these clans sought help from Timurid Zahir al-Din Babur (1526–1530) from Khurasan. After his victory in the Battle of Panipat (1526), Babur established the Mogul Empire in India. Persian was the language used at court and the Persian aesthetic dominated in poetry, calligraphy, and visual art. Babur himself was celebrated for his consummate poems which were known as *Diwan* ("a collection of poems"). His son Humayun (1508–1556) had to assert himself against various opponents and in 1544 even seek temporary refuge in Tabriz at the court of Shah Tahmasp (1524–1576). On his return to India he was accompanied by two Safavid artists: Mir Sayyid Ali (d. c. 1572) and

1798 — French expedition to Egypt under Napoleon Bonaparte; military conquest and scientific investigation of Egypt

1799–1801 — Ottoman army under Muhammad Ali forces the French to leave Egypt

18. UNKNOWN ARTIST

Drawing of a City
Iran, 1400–1450, ink on paper, 13 x 17 cm
Berlin, Staatsbibliothek, Preussischer Kulturbesitz, Oriental Section

19. AQA RIZA

Young Man Day-Dreaming
Iran (Isfahan), around 1590, drawing, ink on paper, 12 x 6.7 cm
Cambridge, MA, Harvard Art Museum, Arthur M. Sackler Museum, Alpheus Hyatt Purchasing Fund, 1952.7

20. ABDALLAH IBN AL-FADL

Astalagus Plant and Hunting Scene Between Animals
In: *Kitab al-Hashaish*, Iraq (Baghdad), 1224 (Abbasid), miniature from a translation of Dioscorides' *De materia medica* (1st century), 19.3 x 16 cm
Istanbul, Ayasofya Museum

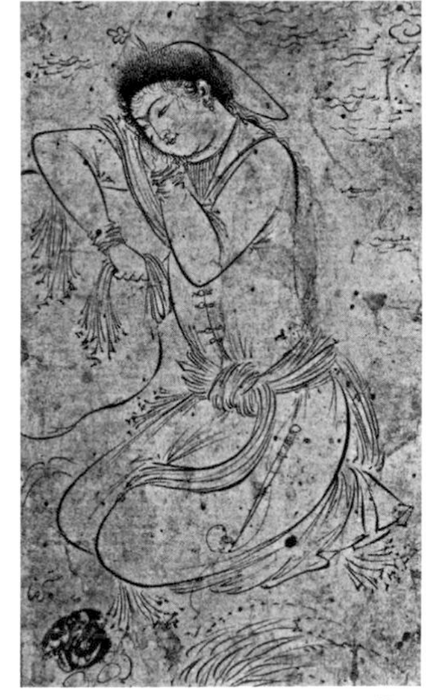

19

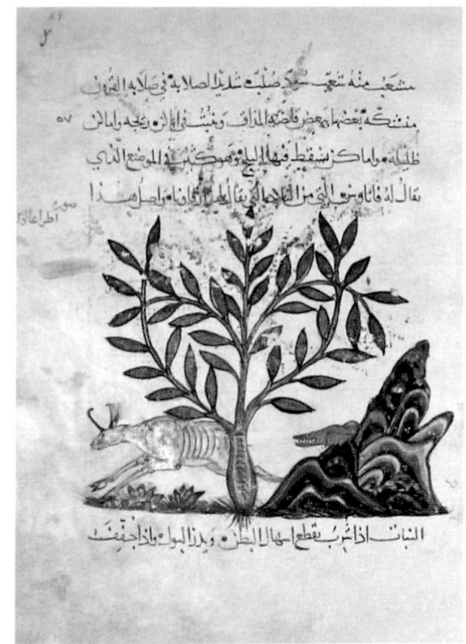

20

Abd al-Samad (active 1540–1595; see ill. p. 90) who are also known from surviving self-portraits. In addition, he brought from Persia several illustrated Timurid manuscripts which were then made available as models for painters in Delhi. Study of these manuscripts and the input of the two Persian artists were to provide lasting inspiration for painting's development at the Mogul court.

Akbar I (1556–1605) enlarged and stabilized the empire, thanks to the tolerance he showed towards Hindus. Thus came into existence a Hindu-Muslim mixed culture, which also shaped the visual arts. Simultaneously, trade routes to Europe were opened up, and from 1580 India became a frequent destination for European legations. Sometimes the European art that reached India in this way had an influence on local developments.

At Akbar's court many works by former Persian poets were copied and illustrated. These included Ibn al Muqaffa's *Kalila wa Dimna* ("Kalila and Dimna"), Firdawsi's *Shahnama* ("Book of Kings"), the *Diwan* by Hafiz (d. 1390), Nizami's (1141–1209) *Khamsa* ("Five Stories"), and also Sultan Babur's autobiography. From around 1562 an extensive manuscript of the *Hamzanama* ("Story of Hamza") was produced, embellished with 1,400 full-page paintings (ill. p. 89). Completion of this manuscript took around 15 years, so its miniatures offer a good survey of the development of 16th century Mogul painting. The oldest depictions still belong to the tradition of Safavid Persian art and were probably done by both the artists Sultan Barbur brought from Tabriz to Delhi. The later pictures already present a more autonomous style.

Alongside illustrations for large-scale projects, individual sheets were produced, showing courtly existence in Delhi with all its ceremonies and receptions. Flemish woodcuts were also used as models for the depiction of Europeans, so that Christian motifs sometimes entered into the pictures of Mogul artists.

The style of Indian Islamic painting that developed at Akbar's court school is characterized by its gentle, nuanced coloring. The persons depicted are graphically embodied, landscapes have a high horizon providing depth, and representations of architecture are spatial and three-dimensional.

Akbar's successors Jahangir (1605–1627) and Shah Jahan I (1627–1658) were also patrons of art. Jahangir was particularly interested in portraits and animal studies, preferring the style of such Persian painters as the previously mentioned Mir Musavvir. He commissioned the bringing together of many individual sheets by famous artists in picture-albums. That custom was also cultivated by Shah

1805–1848 — Muhammad Ali rules in Egypt and modernizes the country influenced by Western ideas
1808–1839 — In Turkey reforms under Mahmud II,
1814 — Iranian-British Treaty strengthens British influence in Iran

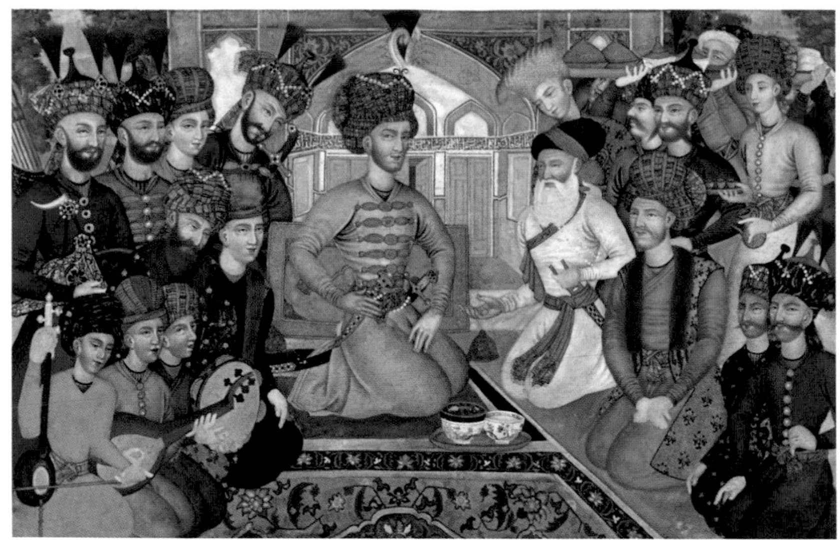

21

Jahan who otherwise only had a few manuscripts produced and is mainly known for construction of the Taj Mahal (1632–1647) as a grave for his favorite wife Mumtaz Mahal ("The Chosen One of the Palace"). After the death of Shah Jahan the quality of Mogul painting declined since his son Aurangzeb (1658–1707) was for religious reasons somewhat dismissive of the arts. He banned music at court, discharged painters, and had only one really important building erected: the chief mosque at Lahore. His war campaigns against the Maratha in Central India and the Deccan Sultanates led to corruption and dissolution of the administrative structure. After Delhi had been conquered in 1739 by the Iranian Nadir Shah Afshar (1736–1747), the Mogul Empire broke up into a loose grouping of states which existed until the 19th century.

Many works by Mogul artists reached the West from the 18th century onwards as a result of close political relations with Europe. Book illustrations, carpets, textiles, and works incorporating jewels and metal were greatly admired and viewed as providing models for European crafts. In 1856 Owen Jones, the British art theoretician and architect, expressed his appreciation of Indian ornamentation as follows: "This meticulous design-process becomes apparent in all works by Indians ... There are neither excrescences nor superfluous ornamentation. Everything serves a purpose and nothing could be taken away without impairing the composition".

Art in the Ottoman Empire

While the Timurid, Safavid, and Mongol dynasties dominated Eastern Islamic regions, the Ottomans came to power in the area that is today's Turkey. As early as 1281 Osman I (Osman Ghazi; 1281–1324) established the first Ottoman kingdom in Bithynia (the area around Bursa), attracting many followers after his victory over a Byzantine army. His son Orhan (1324–1360) captured Iznik and his grandson Murad I (1362–1389) Adrianopel (Edirne), allowing the Ottomans to institute their rule over Asia Minor. The conquest of Constantinople in 1453 by Mehmed II, Fatih ("the Conqueror"; 1444–1446 and 1451–1481) sealed the end of the Byzantine Empire. Ottoman dominance spread continuously in the centuries that followed. After occupying the Eastern Mediterranean and Egypt, Ottoman armies took possession of North Africa (1534–1574) and in the 17th century advanced towards Eastern Europe. Despite defeats at Lepanto (1571) and at the Gates of Vienna (1683), the Ottomans stabilized their rule

1821 — State printing house established in Cairo

1830 — The French occupy Algeria

1832 — Appearance of the first Ottoman newspaper

21. UNKNOWN ARTIST

Shah Abbas II Receives the Indian Ambassador
Iran (Isfahan), c. 1663, opaque watercolors, gold on paper, glued on blue card, 20 x 31.4 cm
Geneva, Aga Khan Trust for Culture

22. MU'IN MUSAVVIR

Double Portrait of Nawab Mirza Muhammad Baqir and his Son Mirza Husayn
Iran (Isfahan), 1674, opaque watercolors on paper, 13.6 x 24 cm
Geneva, Aga Khan Trust for Culture

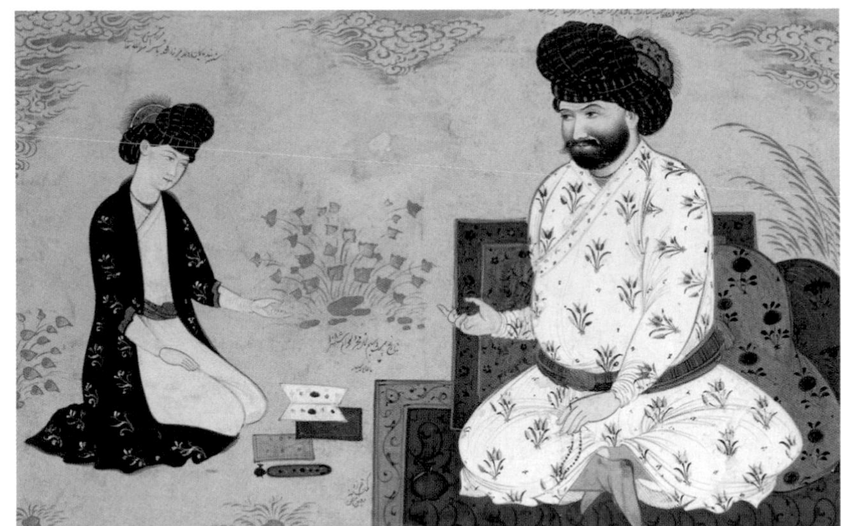

22

and constituted an important Islamic counterweight to the European Great Powers until the 19th century.

The Sultans favored a luxurious lifestyle and cultivated an interest in architecture and the visual arts. Their patronage of art was comparable with that of European rulers. After conquest of Byzantine areas there were lively artistic exchanges with the West and also intensive relations with India. Ottoman art thus developed within the frictions engendered by a great diversity of traditions. In Europe it was much admired and – especially in Italy – much imitated. The court workshop in Constantinople designed the elaborate monograms (ill. p. 25) which every Sultan used for signing official documents. Alongside calligraphy and paintings the workshop also produced designs for ornamentation of textiles, ceramics, and tiles used in royal buildings and mosques. The perfectionism of its great influence over painting soon led to a degree of formalism and stagnation, while ceramics flourished (ills p. 82, 83). The Guild of Ceramic Artists thus manifested great self-assurance when presenting its wares during the craftsmen's procession for Murad III (1574–1595) in Constantinople's Hippodrome (ill. p. 24 left).

Ottoman ceramics had developed out of an attempt to imitate Chinese porcelain, especially the blue-and-white ware of the Yuan (1279–1368) and Early Ming (1368–1643) periods, which had been imported into the Islamic world since the second half of the 14th century. Between 1480 and 1550 potteries in Iznik and Kutahya elaborated an autonomous style. Their products were characterized by a rich variety of styles and motifs which were constantly improved. Especially popular was ornamentation in what was known as the *Quatre Fleurs* style, devised in the 1530s, with its realistic yet two-dimensional and sometimes freely colored representation of roses, carnations, tulips, and hyacinths (ill. p. 82). In the late 18th and 19th centuries European models became more influential and an Oriental-Western mixed style came into existence, reflecting the Ottoman Empire's opening to the West.

Persian Art under the Qajars

Between 1779 and 1925 Persia was ruled by the Qajars, a Turkmen Dynasty from the Qizilbash tribe based in the North of the country. The art now produced fluctuated between continuation of existing traditions and openness to new developments, above all to European models. The extent of Qajar rulers' responsiveness to moderni-

1839–1861 — Expansion of reform policies (Tanzimat) in the Ottoman Empire

1841 — Muhammad Ali becomes hereditary Vizier of Egypt; recognition of Ottoman supreme power

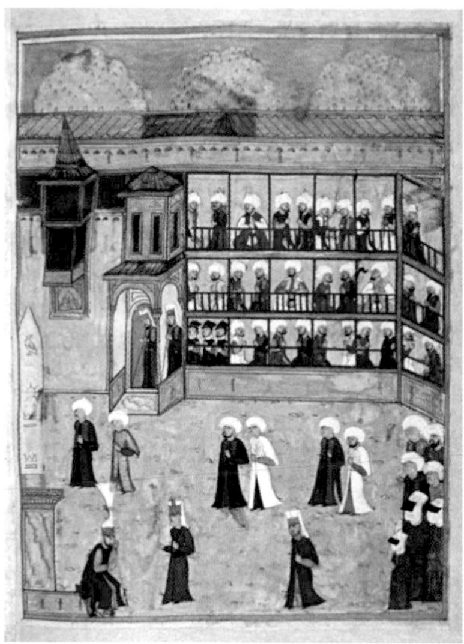

23

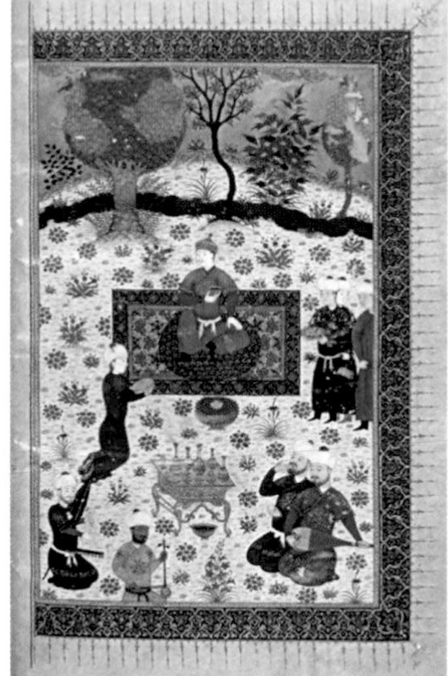

24

23. THE GUILD OF POTTERS (ÇÖMLIKÇILER)

Parading Before Sultan Murad III at the Hippodrome
In: *Surnama* of Murad III, Turkey (Istanbul), c. 1582 (Ottoman), miniature, height 33.7 cm
Istanbul, Topkapi Palace Museum

24. SHAMS AL-DIN BAISUNGHURI

Baisunghur ibn Shahrukh Sitting in a Garden (left-half)
Afghanistan (Herat), October 1429 (Timurid), miniature in a *Kalila wa Dimna* manuscript by Nizamuddin Abu'l-Ma'ali Nasrullah for his monarch Baisunghur ibn Shahrukh, opaque watercolors, ink, and gold on paper, 28.7 x 19.7 cm
Istanbul, Topkapi Palace Museum

ty was demonstrated in visits by Nasir al-Din Shah (1848–1896) to World Fairs at Vienna and Paris in 1873, 1878, and 1889.

In painting, Persian book-art was used for inspiration, but so too was a new, more modeled style – stimulated by Western art – which mainly transformed figurative depiction. The Qajar court workshop produced prestigious full-length portraits of potentates, often as presents for European heads of state. These were intended to present a particular image of the power and greatness of Persian rulers. Fath Ali Shah (1797–1834) saw himself as inheritor of the traditional Persian Greater Kingdom and had seen himself represented accordingly in paintings and frescos, depicting many castles. The Shah thus created an artificial reality, the impact of which was to be felt in public awareness until deep in the 20th century.

A struggle between the old and the new was also to be observed in handicrafts. Many traditional craft techniques vanished and new forms of production were taken over from Europe (partly by European firms operating in Persia). New materials and techniques also contributed to this development, as exemplified by elegantly shaped glass rose-water sprinklers (ill. p. 95) – a completely autonomous Persian 19th-century innovation. On the other hand, art objects were frequently made in a traditional style using long-established techniques so as to be able to sell these products in Europe, where Islamic art was esteemed as a model for national crafts.

A late 19th-century tile from Tehran (ill. p. 8) makes clear how Qajar art gave rise to a kind of "Persian historicism". It shows Jamshid, a mythological ruler mentioned in Firdawsi's *Shahnama*, clad in the robes of an Achaemenid (Old Persian) ruler. Before him stand armed men and a servant whose face is veiled so as not to contaminate the Great King with his breath. The throne on which Jamshid is sitting is also based on ancient depictions on reliefs at Persepolis dating from the 6th century BC.

Modern Art

In the 19th and 20th centuries far-reaching political and economic changes shaped the history of the Islamic world, resulting in a breach with traditions in all spheres of art. This development was mainly the outcome of Oriental artists having greater contact with the culture and art of the West. For instance, in Turkish art from the 1930s to the 1960s, there was great openness to European and North American models, accompanied by development of a new formal lan-

1854–1863 — Muhammad Said as Khedive of Egypt; first European loans which lead to financial ruin for Egypt and the Ottoman Empire
1869 — Opening of the Suez Canal

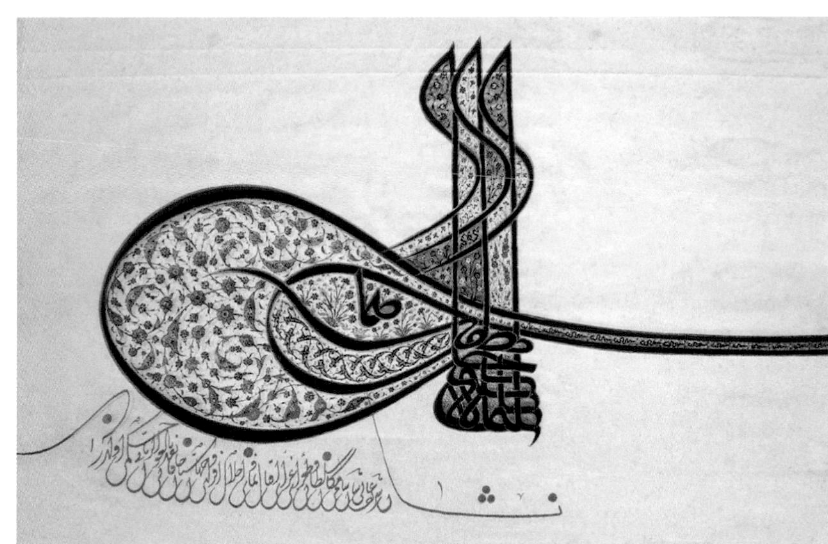

25. FERMAN WITH TUGHRA
Written command from a Sultan with calligraphic representation of the Sultan's name heading official documents, from Sultan Suleyman I ("The Magnificent"), Turkey (Istanbul), April 1552 (Ottoman), paper-roll, document written in *Divani* script, golden and blue ink, 168 x 41 cm (detail)
Istanbul, Topkapi Palace Museum

25

guage in accordance with Western modernism. On the other hand, a striving towards a return to local traditions was always also present in Islamic countries. That is particularly apparent in North Africa where in many places an autonomous art arose, independent of academies and colleges. This painting is based on local folk art and frequently involves representation of everyday life.

In the second half of the 20th century, endeavors towards a revival of the "Islamic" in art were intensified. Efforts were made to find forms and content providing an equivalent of modern Western art. Special importance was assigned to calligraphy which had always been the characteristic achievement of Islamic culture. A fresh interest in using calligraphic forms in painting and sculpture arose, translating Arabic letters into a modern visual language. Widely differing concepts were developed: alongside purely calligraphic composition consisting only of letters, are combinations of calligraphy with figurative motifs and completely abstract utilization of individual elements of script (ill. p. 32). The possibility of using letters and words for a return to the forms of Islamic tradition, while simultaneously transmitting modern content, allows this new art to establish a link between specifically Islamic cultural and historical references and the present day.

1914–1918 — Revolt of the Arabian Peninsula against the Ottoman Empire with support from Lawrence of Arabia (T. E. Lawrence)
1924 — Proclamation of the Turkish Republic under President Mustafa Kemal (Atatürk)

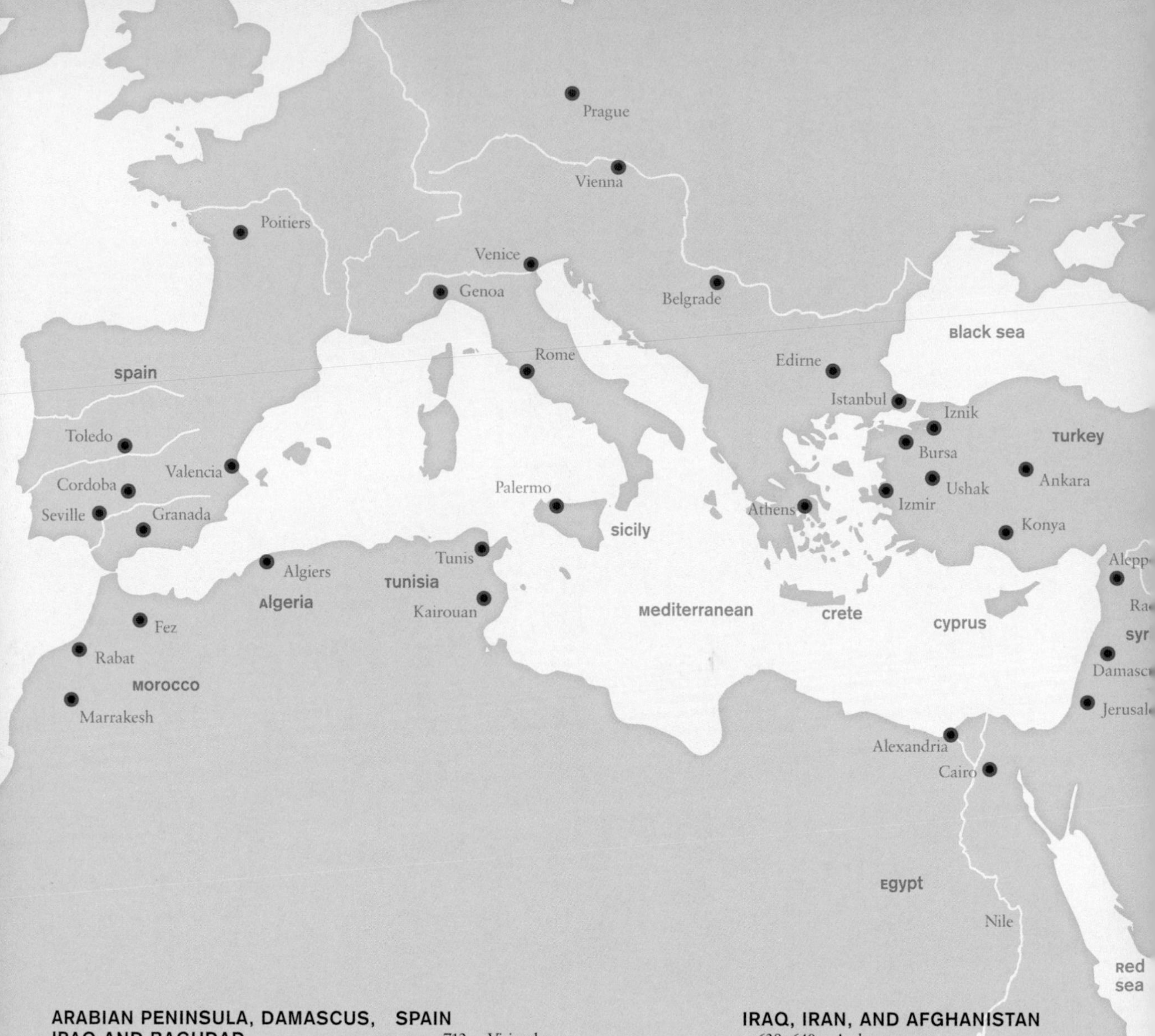

ARABIAN PENINSULA, DAMASCUS, IRAQ AND BAGHDAD

570–632 Muhammad
632–661 First four Caliphs
661–750 Umayyads
749–1258 Abbasids

EGYPT AND SYRIA

868–905 Tulunids
969–1171 Fatimids in Tunisia, Egypt, and Palestine
1171–1250 Ayyubids
1250–1517 Mamluks
1517–1805 Egypt under Ottoman rule

SICILY

827–878 Aghlabids from Tunisia
909–1171 Fatimids

SPAIN

–712 Visigoths
756–1031 Umayyads
1056–1147 Almoravids
1130–1269 Almohads in North Africa and Spain
1232–1492 Nasrids in Granada

NORTH AFRICA

789–921 Idrisids in Morocco
800–909 Aghlabids in Tunisia
1056–1147 Almoravids in Morocco
1228–1534 Hafsids in Tunisia

TURKEY

1077–1327 Rum-Seljuks
1381–1922 Ottomans

IRAQ, IRAN, AND AFGHANISTAN

638–640 Arab conquest
819–1105 Samanids
868–903 Saffarids
1054–1194 Seljuks (unification of Mesopotamia and most of Persia)
977–1186 Ghaznavids
1256–1336 Il-Khans (Ilkhanids)
1378–1502 Qara Qoyunlu and Aq Qoyunlu (Mongols)
1313–1393 Muzaffarids
1340–1432 Jalayirids
1369–1500 Timurids
1501–1732 Safavids
1779–1925 Qajars

INDIA

1206–1555 Delhi Sultanate
1526–1827 Mogul Empire

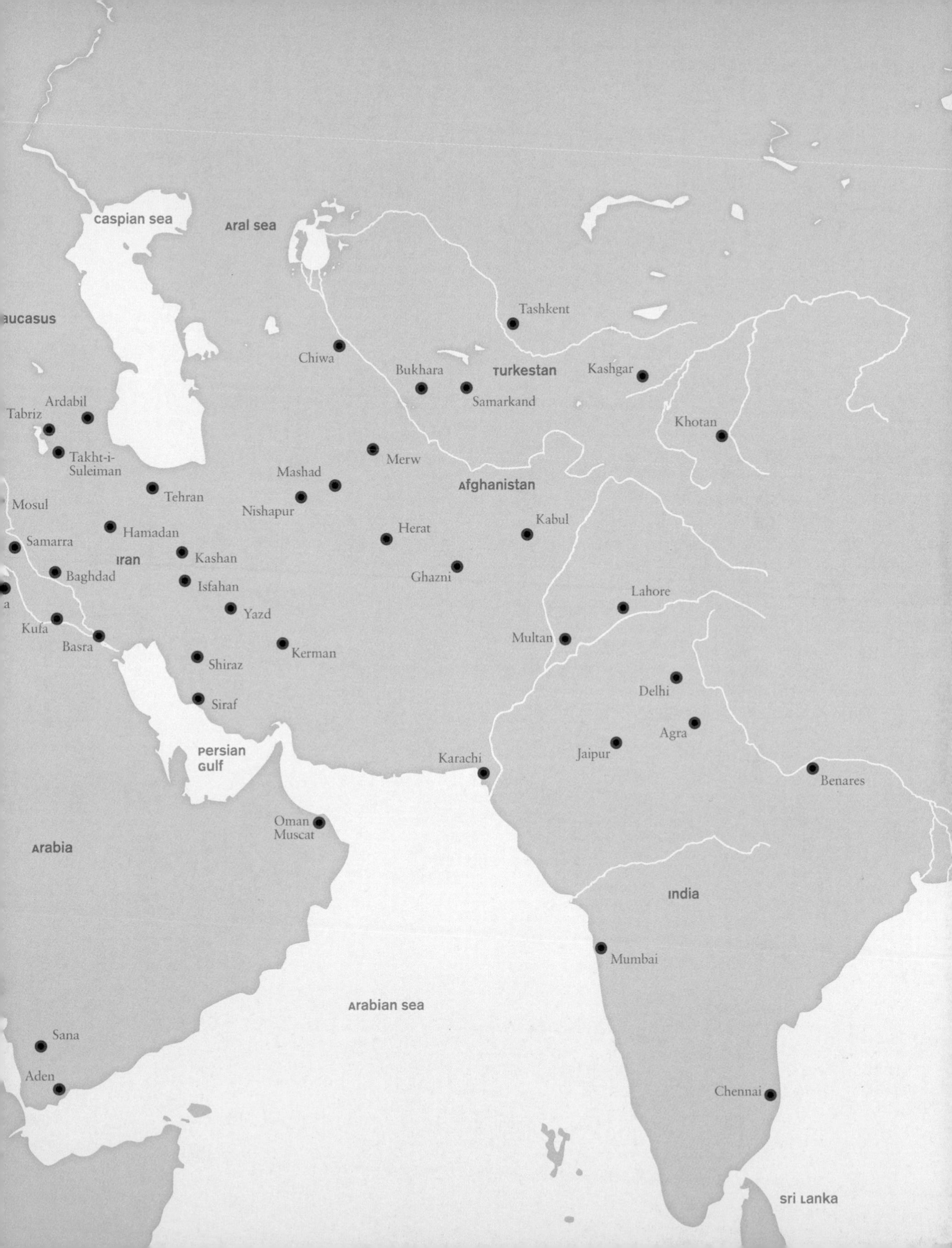

Caspian Sea
Aral Sea
aucasus
Tashkent
Chiwa
Bukhara
Turkestan
Kashgar
Samarkand
Ardabil
Tabriz
Khotan
Takht-i-
Suleiman
Merw
Mashad
Afghanistan
Tehran
Mosul
Nishapur
Kabul
Herat
Hamadan
Samarra
Iran
Kashan
Ghazni
Baghdad
Isfahan
a
Lahore
Yazd
Kufa
Multan
Basra
Kerman
Shiraz
Delhi
Siraf
Agra
Jaipur
Persian
Gulf
Karachi
Benares
Oman
Muscat
Arabia
India
Mumbai
Arabian Sea
Sana
Aden
Chennai
Sri Lanka

Qur'an, Fragment of a Page

Eastern Mediterranean, ink, opaque watercolors, gold on parchment, 23.9 x 33.6 cm
Washington, DC, Freer Gallery of Art

The page from a Qur'an shown here was written in Early Abbasid script in the monumental *Kufic* style named after the Iraqi city of Kufah. Characteristic of *Kufic* is its angularity with the script written from right to left, using a reed pen and brown-black ink, and always with the same distance between individual letters. Red dots serve as indications of vowels. Particularly precious Qur'ans, like this one, are embellished with gold (illumination) with foliation emphasizing the beginning of a new Sura or an entire ornamented page. This page is the left-hand side of a six-line Qur'an manuscript. The first three lines of the text are devoted to verses 87 and 88 from Sura 38, which bears the name *Sad* ("S"). A little palmette in the second line, given emphasis by its color, separates the two verses, and six golden dots in the form of a triangle conclude verse 88 in the third line. The fourth line is accentuated by rectilinear illumination and white lettering against a background embellished in gold with the title of Sura 39, "The Gatherings", standing out here as a heading. In the left-hand margin the palmette-adorned illumination in the second line becomes a tree with symmetrical leaf-shapes. Floral motifs from pre-Islamic Persian art, still influential in 9th-century Iran and Iraq, are deployed here. The first verse of Sura 39 is introduced by a *Bismallah,* which precedes Suras with the invocation "In the name of God, the Compassionate, the Merciful", spoken by a Muslim before undertaking many everyday actions.

In the Islamic world the Qur'an is viewed as a revelation directly from God, so in this culture the written word is of the greatest significance. Reading and writing are inseparably linked with this religion and faith. In religious texts assuring correct transmission was of exceptional importance, but difficulties were frequently produced by Arabic script's distinctive feature of only recording consonants. That is why in Qur'anic manuscripts vowels are indicated by dots, and diacritic marks and other aids to reading are added, enabling clear identification and correct pronunciation of words.

Scholars devised special demarcations of a page for the structuring of Qur'anic manuscripts, and gave precise instructions about the way in which individual letters should be ordered. These were often richly and colorfully ornamental with much gold. Very luxurious manuscripts could be up to 50 x 75 cm in size. Representatives of the ruling class often donated such splendid Qur'ans to mosques.

The art of Islamic book design attained an initial peak in the 9th century. At that time Arabic calligraphy had already become an autonomous art. Additional forms of script, alongside *Kufic* and cursive, were developed from the 10th century onwards.

"One day my script will remain when I have long been dead, my fingers perhaps already decomposed and my hand gone for ever."

Anonymous, Arabic, 16th/17th century

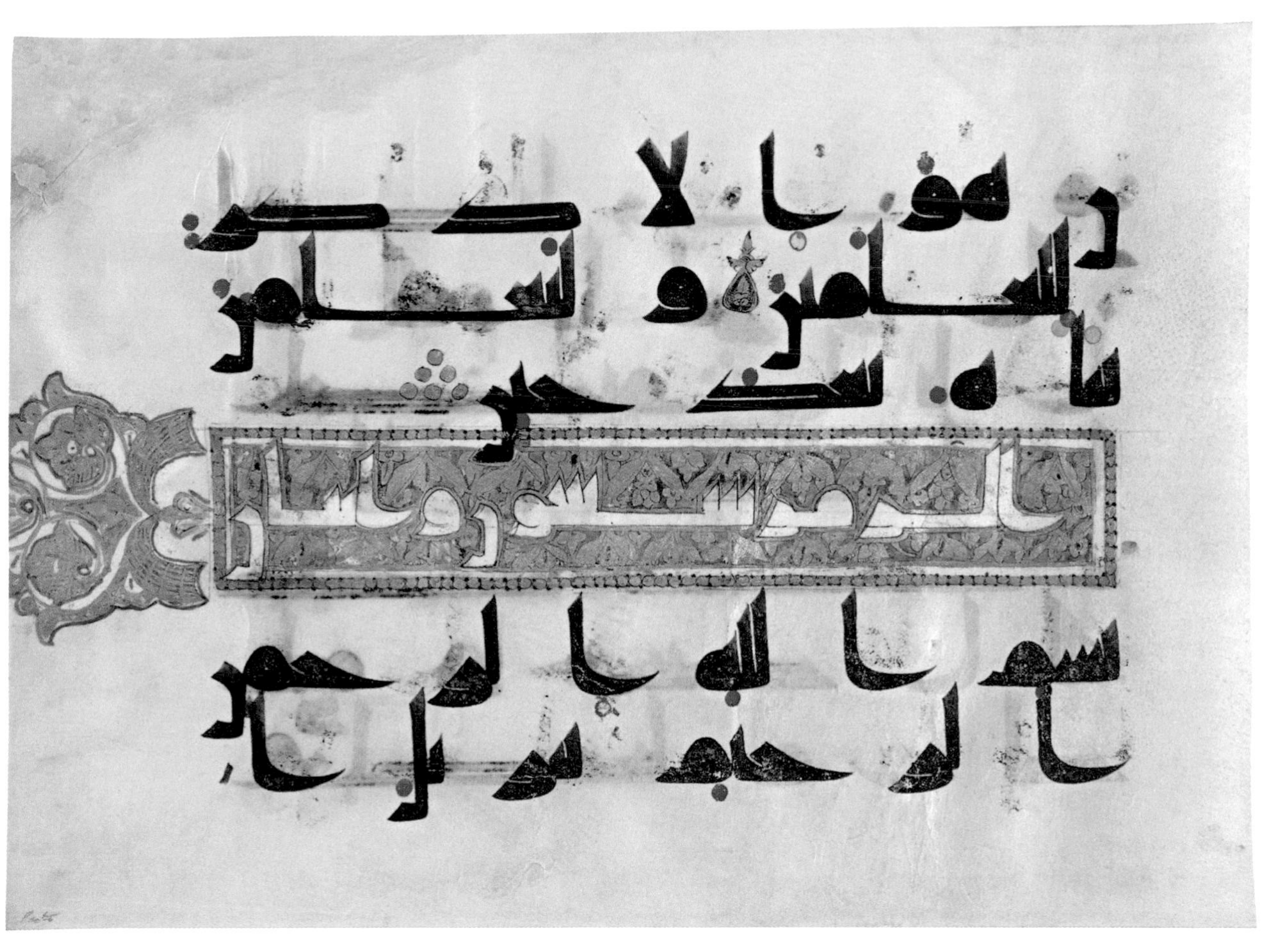

Two Women Dancers with Wine Bottles

Iraq (Samarra), wall fresco, from the domed room in the audience hall of the Dar al-Khalifa (Caliph's Palace) Reconstruction by Ernst Herzfeld, 1913, 50 x 50 cm

Conflicts between Turkish mercenaries in their service led the Abbasid Dynasty to leave Baghdad and in 836 establish a new capital at Samarra, around 150 km to the North. A city was constructed on a previously unsettled area over 20 km in length with several royal palaces and other buildings for the administration and court officials.

The depiction shown here is the reconstruction of a fresco from the Caliph's Palace which has only survived in a very bad state. The remaining fragments are today in Istanbul's Museum of Turkish and Islamic Arts. Ernst Herzfeld, who excavated the palace, recognized that two dancing women with wine bottles are depicted here and completed the image accordingly.

Each of the two women, facing one another, holds translucent, bottle-like vessels with one hand high above her head, while elegantly pouring wine from this receptacle into a shallow golden bowl in the other hand. In the lower part of this representation a small and compressed section of the landscape can be recognized between the two women.

These two women are expensively dressed with skirts down to their feet and long-sleeved blouses. Stoles cover their upper arms. Their rich robes are depicted in a highly stylized way so that the folds are almost transformed into ornamentation. The hairstyles accord with 9th century fashion: a fringe, restrained curls, and long plaits reaching down to the hips. Pearls adorn their hair, headdress, and earrings. The two women's almond-shaped eyes accord with the oriental ideal of beauty whereas their slightly angular faces are closer to Iranian characteristics as found in the art of the Sassanid period (224–651).

The motif of women dancers with wine bottles and scarves in their hands was originally developed in Iranian Sassanid art. From the 8th century onwards this became part of the repertoire of themes in traditional Islamic court art. The early Abbasid courts were famous for their extravagant and sometimes dissolute lifestyle, which included music, dance, riding competitions, and wrestling. Time and again references to their festivities appear in both the visual art and the poetry of that time. For instance, Abu Nuwas (757–815) wrote: "The wine went the rounds among us in a golden beaker, emblazoned by Persia with diverse images." That quotation makes clear that rulers and their retinue frequently ignored the Qur'anic prohibition of wine. The verse also reveals the extent to which the culture and art of pre-Islamic Iran still exerted an influence in the 9th century.

In his book *The Paintings of Samarra* (1927), Ernst Herzfeld quoted a poem by his contemporary Rainer Maria Rilke (from *The Book of Poverty and Death*, 1903), testifying to the culture of the archaeologist in charge of excavating Samarra between 1911 and 1913: "For there are gardens, created by Kings who briefly took pleasure there with young women, enhancing with flowers the wondrous sound of their laughter."

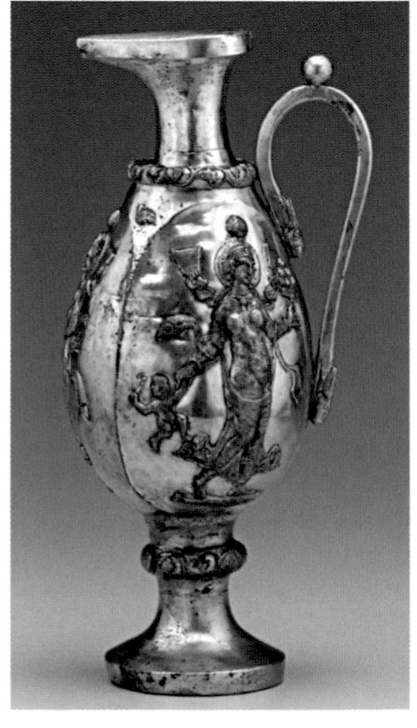

Ewer, Iran, 6th–7th century

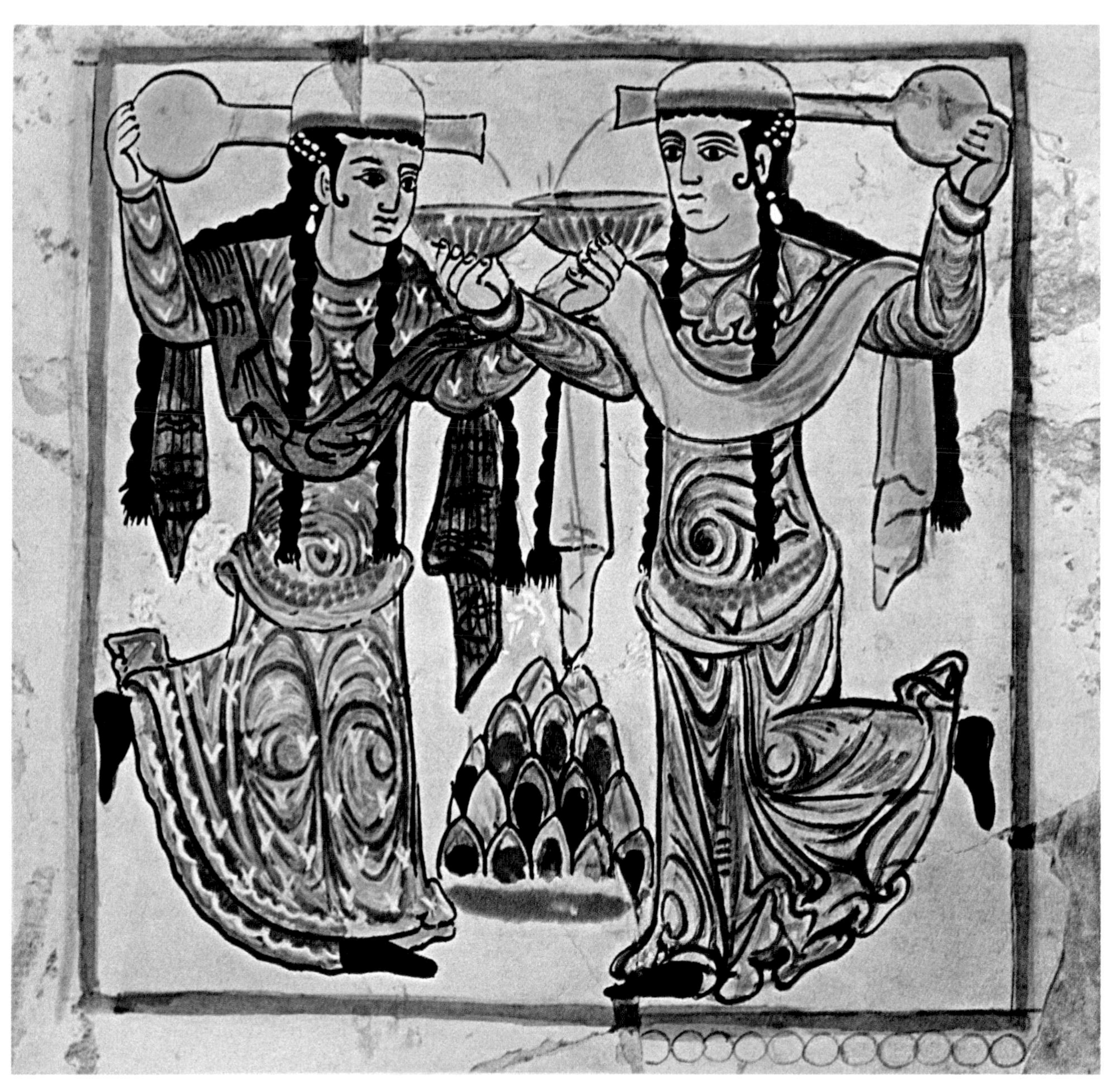

Bowl with inscription

North-East Iran, fired red ceramic with white coating and black painting beneath a transparent glaze, 33.8 cm in diameter
Paris, Musée du Louvre

Luminously primed ceramics were produced in East Iran around 950 and later found during excavations in the city of Nishapur. Similar wares were also made at Afrasiab (Old Samarkand) in Central Asia.

The bowl is decorated with an inscription in *Kufic* script: "The taste of knowledge is first bitter, but finally sweeter than honey." That is followed by the wish for "Health" [for the bowl's owner]. The inscription is elegant and extended with letters extended upwards and downwards, pointing towards the center of the bowl and thereby establishing a relationship with a dot there. Differentiation of the form and height of letters adds a rhythmic element to the surface of the bowl but a large area was left free in the middle. The high quality indicates that excellent calligraphers wrote this inscription, possibly inspired by models in contemporary Qur'an manuscripts. Calligraphers in potters' workshops developed an elegant style harmoniously adapted to each particular piece. Their best work, as here, belongs among the aesthetically most outstanding achievements in Islamic ceramics. The local population may have spoken Persian, but had been familiar with the language of the Qur'an ever since adoption of Islam around 640. Arabic script gained acceptance after the Islamic conquest of Iran. Bowls embellished with Arabic inscriptions were thus appreciated even though the text was not easy to read.

The ornamentation was applied to a clay slip coating. In this technique a white impermeable engobe was poured over the unfired bowl (or else the bowl was submerged in the clay slip); and then the bowl was painted and covered with a transparent glaze. Iranian ceramicists used this in an attempt to imitate Chinese white china from the Sung period (960–1279), which had been imported into the Middle East since the Early Middle Ages. Muhammad ibn al-Husain thus reported in 1059 that the former Governor of Khurasan presented Harun al-Rashid (786–809) with 20 pieces of the most precious Chinese porcelain, said to be more beautiful than anything previously known at the court of the Caliphs. From such Chinese models Persian artists developed this new kind of ceramics with a quality and aesthetic completely its own. However, such ceramics were only produced for a brief period.

Even today applications of calligraphy still play an important part in the art of the Islamic world. Various painters deploy individual Arabic letters in their works, create abstract patterns from written motifs, or combine calligraphic elements with diverse abstract forms.

Wijdan, Ala Allah, 1993

"Arabic calligraphy appeals to Muslim aesthetics which are traditionally linked with writing, above all for Arabs whose main form of art, ever since the pre-Islamic period, has been poetry. So artists can show through written signs what they cannot express by way of figurative depiction."

Wijdan, Amman, 2005

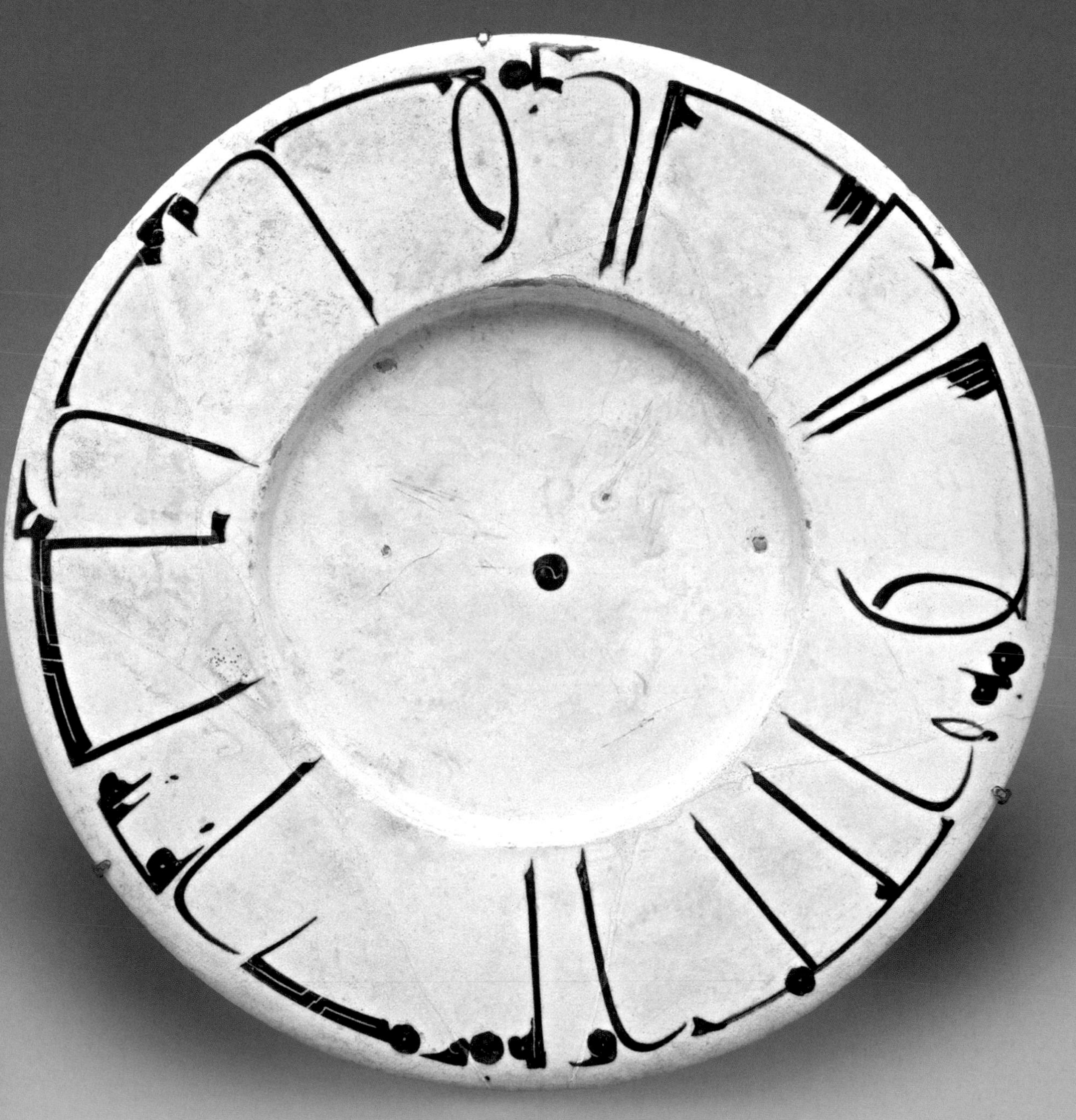

Bowl

Egypt, ceramic, lusterware, diameter 26.1 cm, height 6.7 cm
Washington, DC, Freer Gallery of Art

Under the Fatimid Dynasty in Egypt (973–1171), a striking form of ceramics with glittering metallic surfaces was produced. This extraordinary impression was achieved by what is known as luster technique, a complex manufacturing process originally developed in the 7th and 8th centuries for the decoration of glass, and also applied to ceramics from the 9th century. The already fired and glazed vessel was painted with colors made from metal alloys. Then the painting was fixed during a second firing at lower temperatures (600–900 degrees centigrade), giving the metals a sheen. For this copper, gold, silver, and platinum were pulverized and mixed with other ingredients before being fired for three days, making them suitable for use in painting ceramics.

Lusterware was much admired and the artists who produced it were highly esteemed. That is shown by the painters' signatures preserved on some pottery, and one source also records a competition between two such artists in the 11th century. The fact that the names of those artists were even mentioned shows that an individual style was already appreciated. It is known, too, that rulers owned these precious ceramics. Historian al-Maqrizi (1364–1442) reported (on the basis of older sources) that Caliph al-Mustansir (1036–1094), confronted with difficulties in paying his troops between 1067 and 1069, had to sell the royal treasures at knock-down prices. Luster ceramics are listed among the art objects put up for sale.

Fatimid lusterware was often embellished with figurative scenes from court life – like this bowl depicting a woman dancer between two jugs of wine. The painters were inspired by ancient models, but also took up the local traditions of Coptic craftsmen. Influences from the Iraq of the Abbasid period (749–1258) were also particularly important. Comparison between the vigorously leaping dancer on this bowl with the similar theme in a painting from Samarra (ill. p. 31) makes clear how free and lively Fatimid representations were. As at Samarra, the lady here is richly clothed and holding a scarf. Her face accords with 11th to 12th century ideals of beauty: a straight nose, small mouth, almond-shaped eyes, and finely drawn eyebrows. The shaping of the dancer's face and delineation of her clothing is as vivacious as the representation of her movement.

Non-figurative motifs are also to be found on lusterware, including vine leaves, calligraphy and, as here, stylized palmettes or semi-palmettes.

Unlike many other examples of mediaeval art, it is possible to date Fatimid luster ceramics precisely. Two of the surviving pieces have dated inscriptions from the time of Caliph al-Hakim (996–1021), so that other ceramics can be dated by comparisons of style.

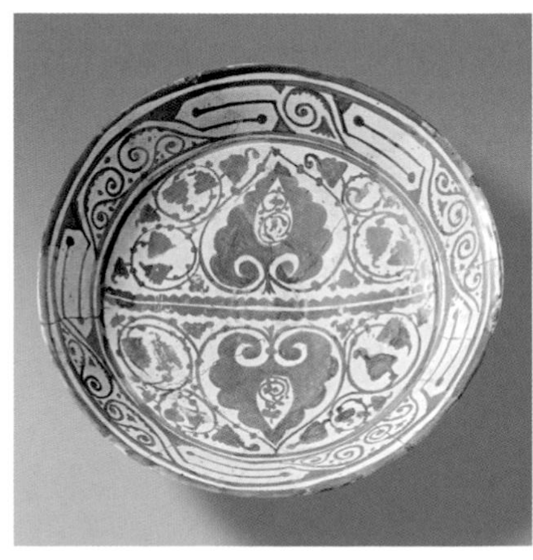

Egyptian ceramicist, Bowl, Egypt (Fustat, Old Cairo), 11th–12th century

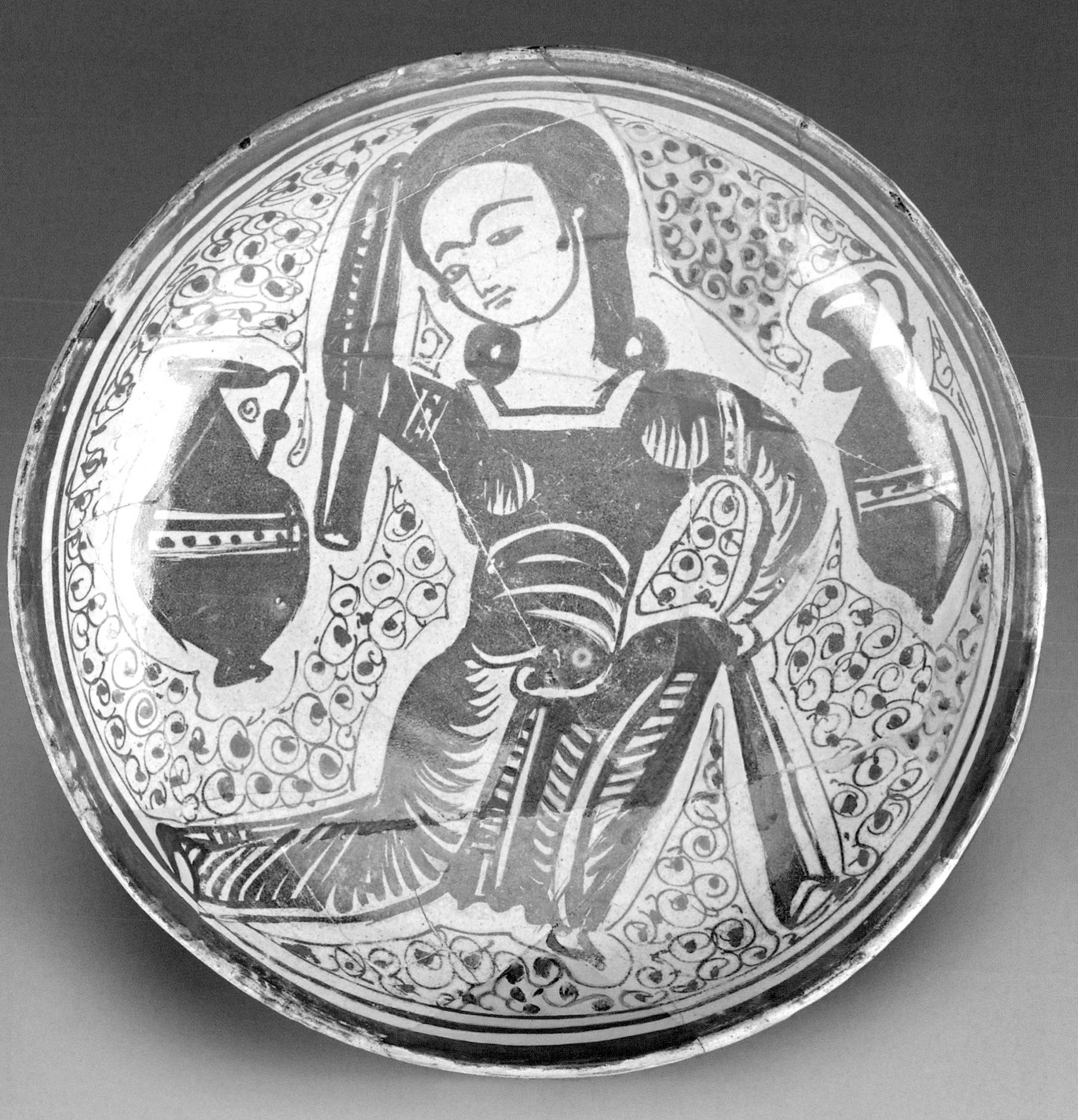

Group of Horsemen Awaiting a Festive Procession

Iraq (Mosul or Baghdad), opaque watercolors and gold, entire page 26.1 x 24.3 cm (detail)
Paris, Bibliothèque nationale de France

This miniature is one of a total of 99 illustrations in a copy of the *Maqamat* ("Assemblies") by Muhammad al-Hariri (1053–1122) from Basra (see ill. p. 39), with both text and pictures produced by Mahmud al-Wasiti. However, where this artist lived and worked still remains unclear up to the present day. The suffix al-Wasiti merely shows that at some stage of his life he was linked with the city of Wasit. Stylistic reasons have long been adduced for locating this manuscript in the capital, Baghdad, but that attribution has not been proven, so the manuscript may have been produced elsewhere. Comparisons can be made with miniatures from a Jacobite Christian manuscript belonging to a monastery close to Mosul (ill. p. 36). Mubarak the Monk recorded that he completed this work in May 1220 in the monastery of Mar Mattai. His illustrations clearly demonstrate the similarities between Christian and Islamic painting in the 13th century.

In his *Maqamat* al-Wasiti copied one of the Islamic world's best-known collections of stories from the Middle Ages. This tells how the crafty al-Harith's powers of persuasion and all kinds of trickery get other people to give him money time and again. The artful language deployed here made this work exceptionally popular in cultivated court circles.

This miniature with the festively adorned group of horsemen relates to the seventh *Maqama*. As the text relates, it is the end of Ramadan, the month of fasting, and the riders are awaiting a procession at Barkaid, north of Mosul. Four of them carry banners with inscriptions, two musicians are blowing long-necked trumpets, and a third is beating a kettle-drum. Behind the men are hanging cloths, bearing inscriptions. The entire group is presented as being pressed closely together with horses and riders staggered behind one another. The banners and musical instruments are arranged in such a way that they point in different directions and almost seem like a geometrical pattern. They thus form an optical counterweight to the somewhat statically conceived animals. A large standard bursts the bounds of the picture, established by the inscription above and below. The fact that the figures are crowded close to the lower edge almost creates the impression that what is happening here is taking place on stage.

The depictions in this manuscript give an extremely detailed representation of life in the 13th century. There are scenes with precisely rendered mosques with minarets, markets, domed bazaars and libraries, and also events on village streets and in cemeteries, in hostelries and schools. All the pictures demonstrate the painter's great sense of certainty in composing scenes, and their coloration with powerful and brilliant emphases reveals al-Wasiti's artistic skills.

Mubarak the Monk, John the Baptist Receives his Name, Iraq (Mar Mattai near Mosul), 1220

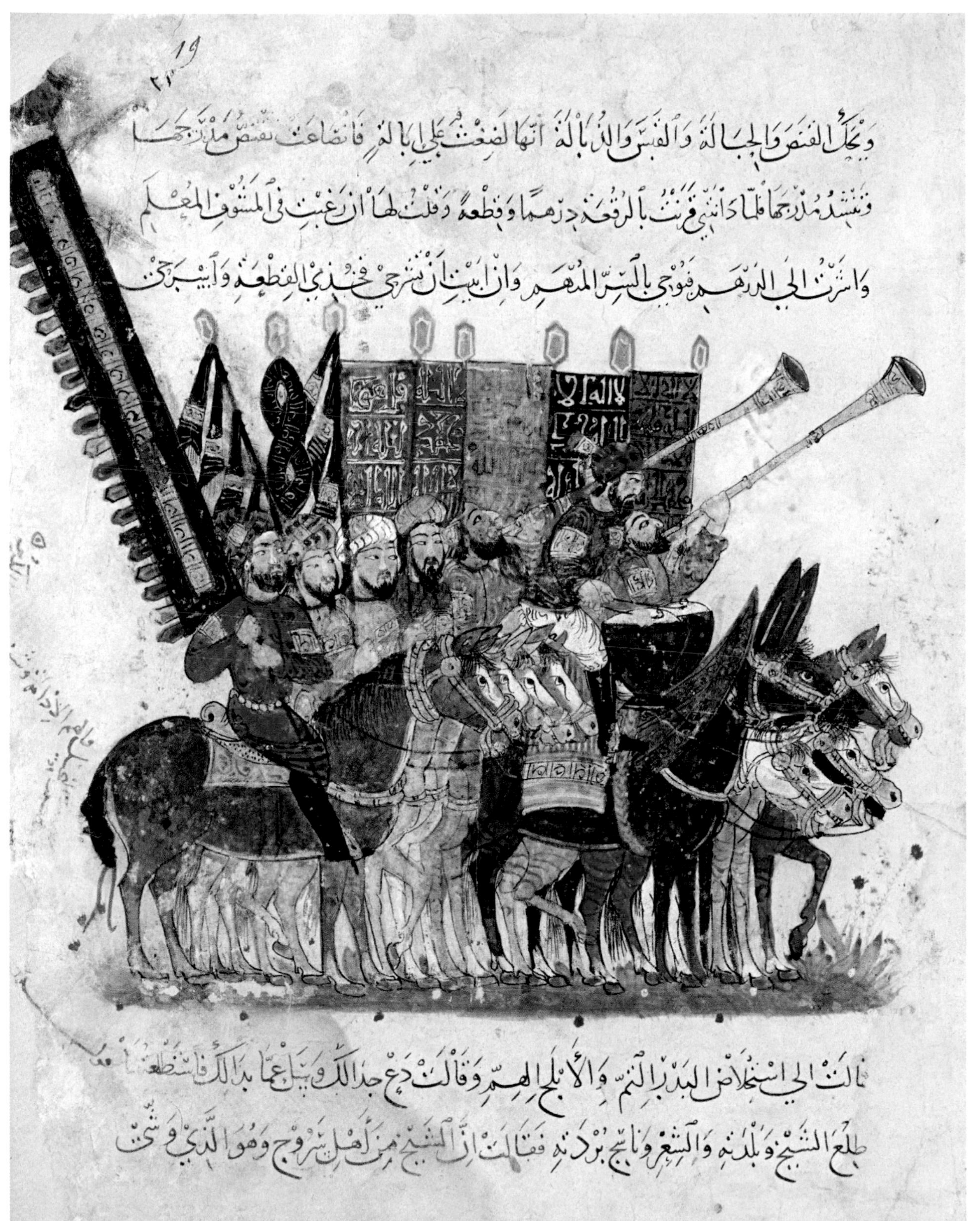

وتحلّ القص والجبالة والقبس والذبالة انها لضغث على ابالة فانصاعت تقتص مدرجها

وتنشد مدرجها فلما دانتني قرنت بالرقعة درهما وقطعة وقلت لها ان رغبت في المشوف المعلم

واشرت الى الدرهم فبوحي بالسر المدهم وان ابيت ان تشرحي فخذي القطعة وابرحي

الت الى استخلاص البدر التم والابلج الهم وقالت دع جدالك وبيّن عما بدا لك فاستطعتها

طلع الشيخ وبلدته والشعر وناسج بردته فقالت ان الشيخ من اهل سروج وهو الذي وشّى

Wedding Meal in a Hostelry

Egypt, ink, opaque watercolors, gold on paper, miniature 15.4 x 12 cm, entire page 37.3 x 26 cm (detail)
Vienna, Austrian National Library

The copy of the *Maqamat* ("Assemblies") texts by Muhammad al-Hariri from Basra (1053–1122, see ill. p. 37) from which this miniature comes, was made by Abu-l-Fada'il ibn Abu Ishaq, in Egypt, probably in Cairo. For a long time it was not known who had painted the 69 miniatures embellishing the text. The one shown here illustrates the 29th *Maqama*, telling of a wedding celebration in a hostelry. In the German translation of these stories, made in 1827 by linguist, orientalist, and poet Friedrich Rückert (1788–1866), the elaborate speech-style used in the Arabic original with many plays on words is very well transposed into another language.

The musicians at this wedding feast in a hostelry, four men and a woman, are shown sitting very close to one another with legs crossed as if the scene is taking place on stage with the curtains pulled to one side. This unreal atmosphere is underlined by the use of gold. On the left, the storyteller, Abu Zaid, can be recognized by his white beard and differently patterned gown. He is toasting another guest, but even though prominently presented is not otherwise emphasized. A woman musician plays a lute adorned with inlays. One of the men touches her mouth. Their robes, characterized by ornamentally stylized folds and tendrils of arabesques, seem like flat ornamentation rather than real textiles. These characters are logically arranged so that the individual figures are related to one another by way of their looks and gestures. The artist deliberately endowed them with a monumental character through their size in relationship to the overall area. He did not seek any depiction in depth so that a tray with a bottle, two glasses, and four fruit-like objects float above the characters. A bottle on the left and a beaker on the right also imply the wedding meal.

This manuscript is exceptionally richly ornamented. Its images are brilliantly colored with frequent use of a golden ground. All of that indicates that this was produced for the Mamluk (1250–1517) court in Cairo, probably under Sultan Hasan ibn Muhammad Nasir al-Din (1347–1351 and 1354–1361). The style is characteristic of a new way of depicting people in book-painting developed at this time, and also used in metalwork and enameled glass. The fact that such a splendid manuscript was produced in response to a royal commission shows that al-Hariri's entertaining stories were also appreciated at court.

"An example of how naively Arabs sometimes sought to circumvent perspective. We observe a meal with guests ... Floating above in the air is the table decoration, a flowerpot. Above this in turn floats a table with the dessert, a bowl with sweets, and the wine. Incapacity in perspectival conjunction of objects is also often amusingly paralleled by Arab painters' lack of skill in other respects."

Josef von Karabacek,
On the Supposed Islamic Ban on Representation, 1876

وانصلت منا انصلات الفرار فأوحشنا فراقه وأدهشنا امراقه
ولم نزل ننشده بكل ناد ونستخبر عنه كل مغد وغاد إلى أن قيل انه مذ
دخل عانة ما زايل الحانة فأغراني خبث هذا القول بسبله والانسلال
فما لبست من سلبه وادلجت الى الدسكرة في هيئة متنكره فإذا الشيخ
في حلة ممصرة بين دنان ومعصرة وحوله سقاة تبهر وشموع تزهر وآس وعبهر ومزمار ومزهر
وهو تارة يستبزل الدنان وطورا يستنطق العيدان ودفعة يستنشق الريحان واخرى يغازل الغزلان

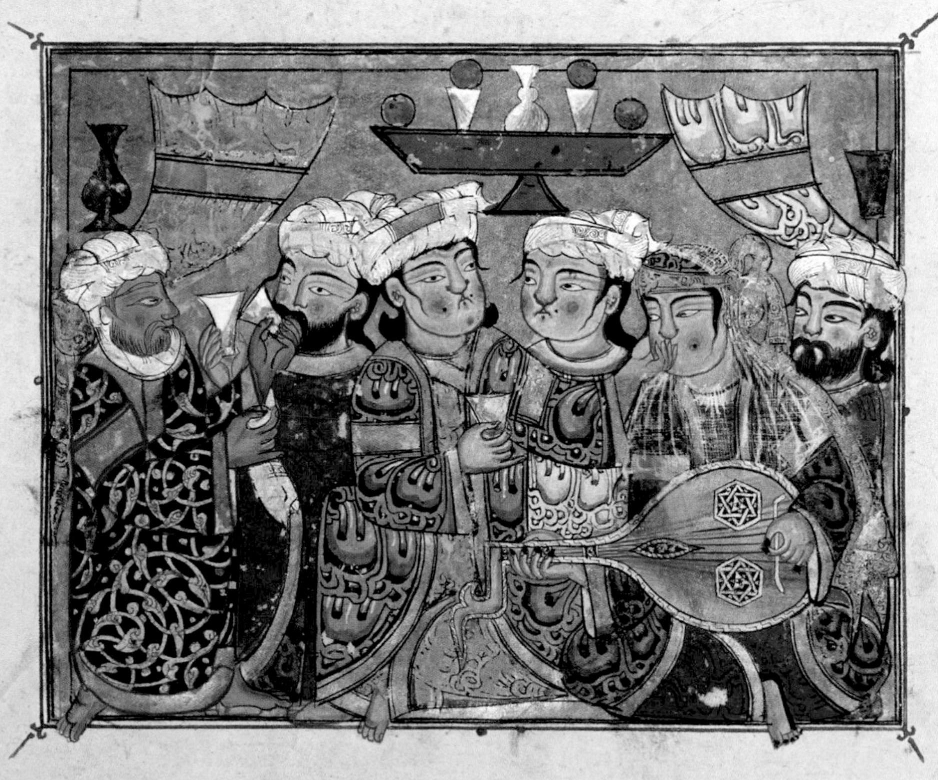

Qur'an: Right-Hand Frontispiece with stellar ornamentation

Egypt (Cairo), paper, decorative lines in gold, blue, white, 75 x 50.5 cm
Cairo, National Library and Archives of Egypt

This one-volume Qur'an was probably originally made for the mosque of Sultan Hassan ibn Muhammad Nasir al-Din (2nd period of rule 1354–1361), which was under construction from 1356. The Sultan died early, so 12 years after the Qur'an was ready it was donated (on 1 June 1368) by Sultan Shaban to the Cairo *madrasa* (school of religious law) headed by his mother, Khawand Baraka. The 413-page text of this Qur'an was the work of Ya'qub ibn Khalili ibn Muhammad ibn Abd al-Rahman al-Hanafi, but the name of the creator of the illuminations (paintings in color) is unfortunately unknown. The right-hand title-page shown here is adorned with an intertwining motif framing three fields of ornamentation. At the centre of each of the two smaller segments, against a background of abundant tendrils of leaves and palmette blossoms, is a cartouche with the words of Sura 56, verses 77 and 78, written on a dark ground: "Surely it is a noble Qur'an in a hidden Book". The central field contains, as the main motif in the entire ornamentation, a 12-pointed star integrated in a continuous interlacing of stellar forms. In the Islamic world the geometry and order of such patterns symbolized the purity and rationality of God as the fundamental aspect of belief. Intertwining of stars were thus to be found in almost all kinds of art from the 10th century. The *minbar* (pulpit in a mosque) with an entrance door and mini-dome – shown here in comparison – provides one example of utilization of geometrical ornamentation. It was part of Sultan Qaitbay's mosque and already seen in the 19th century as an outstanding example of this form of art.

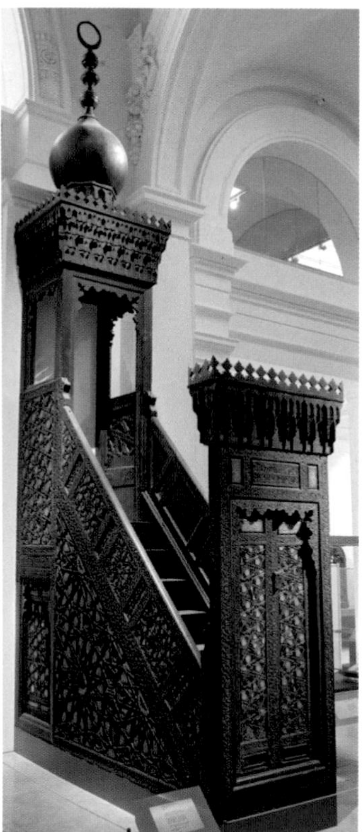

Unknown craftsman in wood, Minbar, Egypt (Cairo), between 1468 and 1496

On this page the stellar entwining are superimposed without creating an impression of three-dimensionality. They are interspersed with floral elements – rosettes, palmettes, and lotus blossoms – which also avoid any impression of embodiment or depth, so that the two-dimensionality of the overall pattern is preserved. In addition, the plant motifs do not affect the predominance of star-like ornamentation. The overall planarity is also upheld by the braiding surrounding the central images, and by the outer framing with palmette blossoms and complex leafy tendrils.

In the 19th century the interweaving of stellar ornamentation and the arabesque with its stylized floral decoration aroused the interest of European artists and theorists of art. Architect Jules Bourguin (1838–1907) thus wrote in 1873 that Arab art was "fundamentally decorative and of importance in the structuring of surfaces" and "exclusively founded on order and geometry." In this system, he maintained, there is no use of elements borrowed from nature; it is complete in itself.

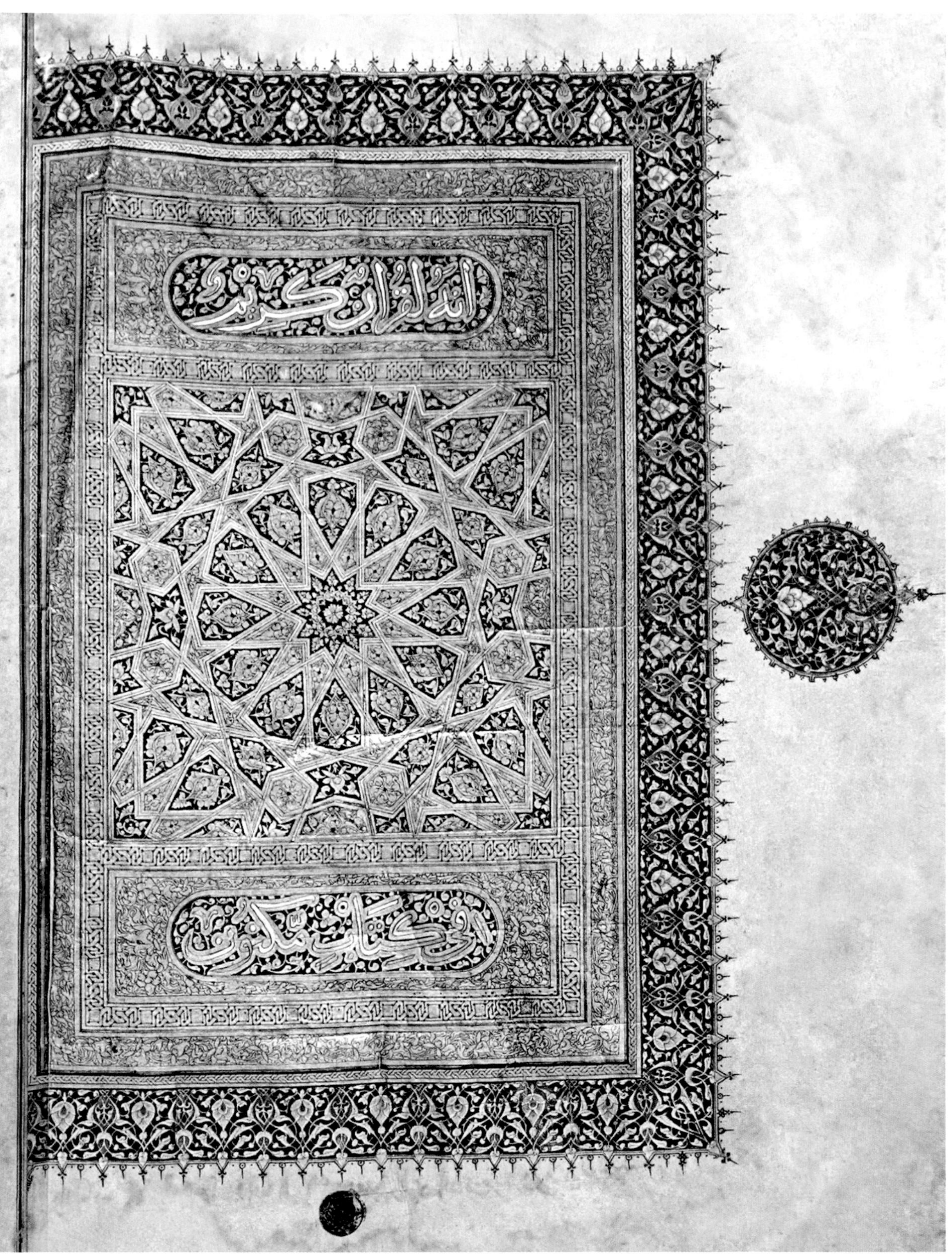
انه لقرآن كريم
في كتاب مكنون

Basin

Egypt or Syria, brass with damascening (silver and gold inlays; some missing), height 23 cm, diameter 50.5 cm
Paris, Musée du Louvre

This large basin was made in the 14th century at the high-point of metalwork in Egypt and Syria. Since the 18th century it has been called the "font of the Holy Louis", linked with King Louis IX (1226–1270) of France. That connection cannot be proved, but it is certain that French royalty were baptized in this basin from the time of Louis XIII (1601–1643) at the latest. It was still used as a font for the baptism of Prince Napoléon-Eugène in 1856.

This basin was produced during the Mamluk period (1250–1517) when Cairo and Damascus were the main centers for precious metal ware. Despite the six inscriptions where the artist's name is mentioned, there is no reference anywhere to the person who commissioned this object, but the high quality of this piece indicates someone from the royal court. Comparison with objects made for Sultan Hasan ibn Muhammad Nasir al-Din (1347–1351, and 1354–1361) suggests that this basin was also created in the mid-14th century.

Depiction of the figures is strikingly monumental and has similarities with the Vienna Hariri manuscript (ill. p. 39). Four medallions show huntsmen on horseback accompanied by courtiers on foot. These men are richly dressed. They wear either turbans or hats (partly East Asian in style) – establishing a distinction between Arabs and Mamluk Turks as participants in the hunt. Some are holding objects indicating their status as holders of high office: director of polo, bearers of swords and bows, master of the wardrobe, the ruler's cupbearer. The huntsmen's clothing consists of tightly fitting jackets, calf-length trousers, riding boots, and sometimes cloaks. Their weapons are swords, bows, or slender lances and spears. Leopards, hawks, and dogs participate in the hunt, and they, like the prey, are reproduced with great accuracy.

On the inner wall of the basin two medallions show enthroned rulers, holding beakers. The artist is probably referring here to a pre-Islamic visual tradition showing the Persian King Khusrau, conqueror of all the evils afflicting the world, with a drinking-glass. Between the medallions huntsmen are to be seen, as on the outer side. The vessel's flat bottom is covered with lively representations of fish and other sea creatures.

Unlike the basin, the richly decorated wooden box, banded by strips of bronze for the safekeeping of a Qur'an manuscript, is covered with purely calligraphic ornamentation, inlaid in silver and gold (some of which is missing). The main element is an extensive inscription with verse 255 (known as the "Throne verse") from Sura 2. The text is in *Thuluth* script ("a third"; see ill. p. 81) from the Mamluk period. Other quotations from the Qur'an in the same script and, also, in *Kufic* are to be found below the main inscription, on the lower edge of the lid, and on the box's sloping surfaces.

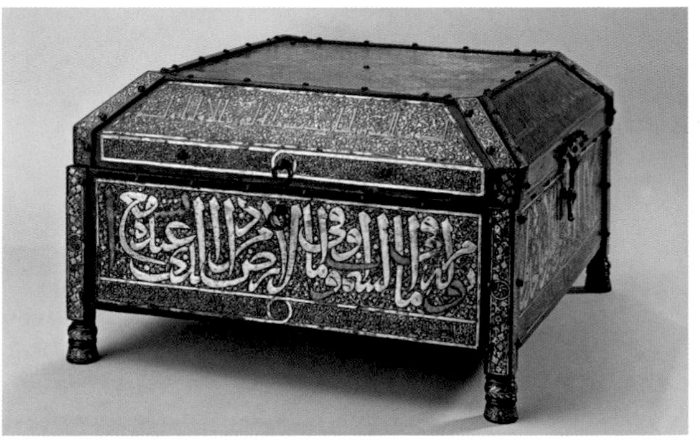

Muhammad ibn Sunqur al-Baghdadi and al-Hadj Yusuf ibn al-Ghawabi, Qur'an Box, Egypt (Cairo), c. 1320–1330

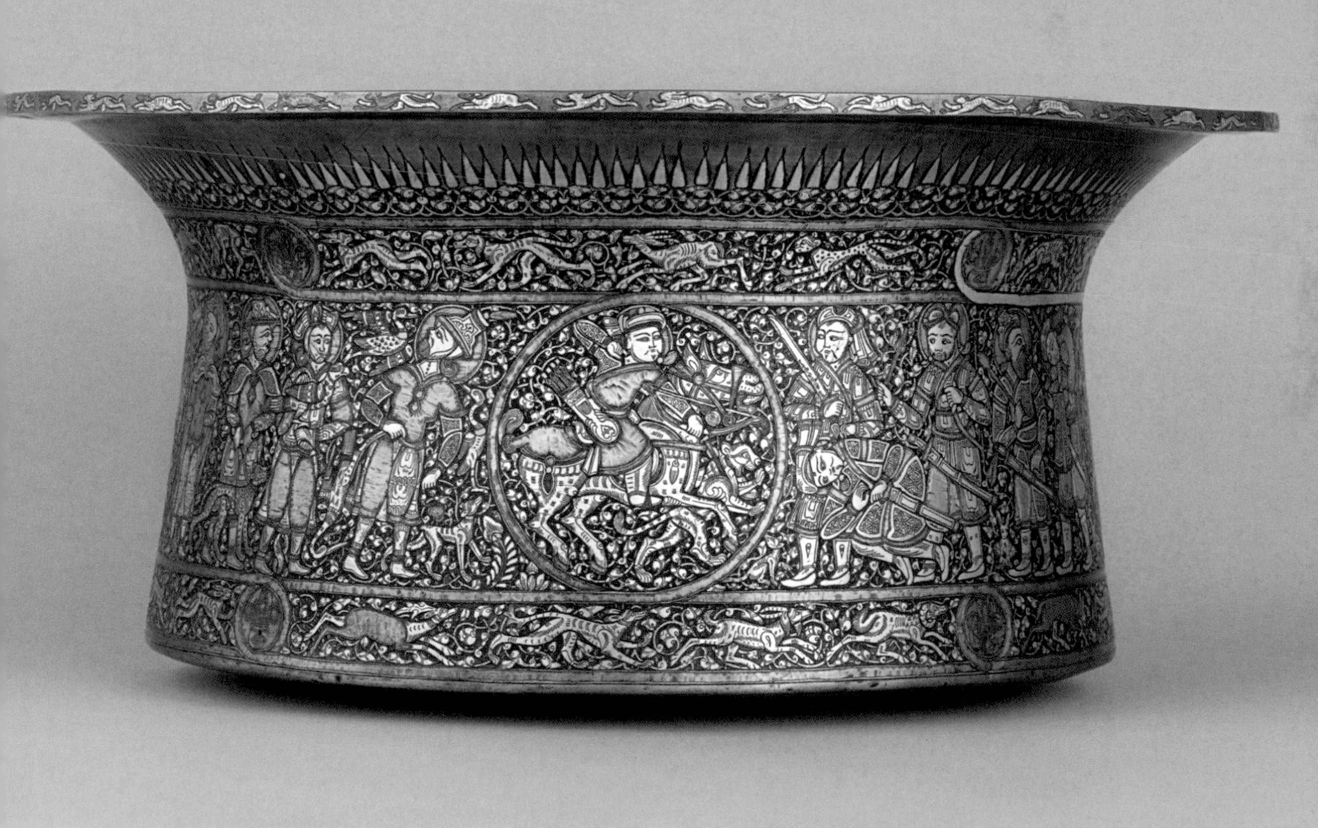

Alhambra vase

Spain (Granada), storage vessel, ceramic, luster-painting, written decoration, height 117 cm
St. Petersburg, Hermitage State Museum

Among the most celebrated examples of Spanish Islamic art are the Alhambra vases, mighty storage vessels with large wing-like handles, the shape of which is reminiscent of *amphorae*. The story of three of the eleven surviving Alhambra vases is closely linked with Mariano Fortuny y Marsal (1838–1874), the famous 19th century Spanish painter and art collector. He also owned this piece. Fortuny discovered it in the parish church at Salar, near Granada in Andalusia, where it was used beneath a stoup. The painter kept this object in his studio, as a painting by Ricardo Madrazo from 1874 shows. After Fortuny's death, the vase was acquired by Prince A. P. Basilevsky for 30,000 Francs, and 10 years later his collection was bought by the Russian government, and this piece ended up in the Hermitage Museum at St. Petersburg.

This vase is adorned with calligraphic inscriptions in a local form of the rectilinear *Kufic* script, characteristic of Granada. The centre of its body is taken up with the word "Health" in dark script on a backing of golden luster, repeated several times as a wish. Above this is a strip of adjacent circles embellished with calligraphy inclusive of the word "Delight". Here the letters are bright, standing out against a dark background. In both of these strips the inscription is enriched with subtle underlying decoration. Beneath the central inscriptions a band of arabesque ornamentation rounds off the adornment of this part of the vase, while above there is another band with white letters against gold-luster. The vase's neck is decorated with geometrical patterns and arabesques.

On the handles is the symbol of "Fatima's Hand" (the Prophet's daughter), traditionally supposed to guard people against the "evil eye". On one side this motif grows out of an area embellished with arabesques and, on the other, out of a calligraphically enhanced form where the word "Well-Being" can be read. In this combination the trees can also be comprehended as a stylized depiction of a tree of life.

The ornamentation of this Alhambra vase reveals Moorish-Spanish craftsmen's liking for calligraphic and geometrical motifs, which were later much admired in Northern and Central Europe from the start of the 19th century.

The principles underlying this art's aesthetic were developed exceptionally early – as is shown by the little ivory box produced in 966 in a studio unconnected with Palace requirements since it was commissioned by someone unknown rather than a courtier. Here too geometrical forms and congratulations are used alongside stylized plants as decoration. This embellishment is very similar to the stucco ornamentation of Medina al-Zahra started in 936.

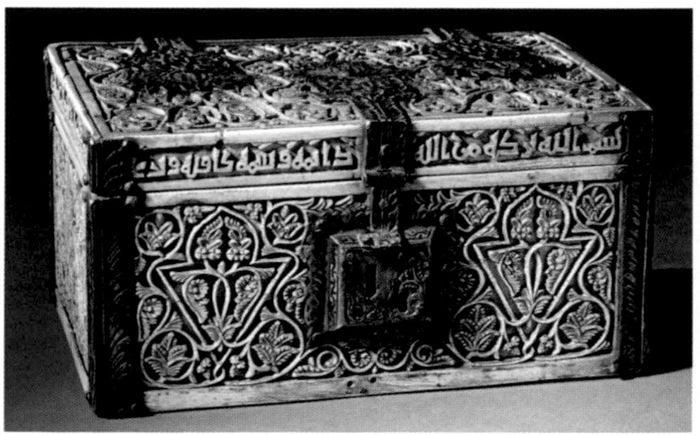

Box with Lid, Spain (Medina al-Zahra), 966

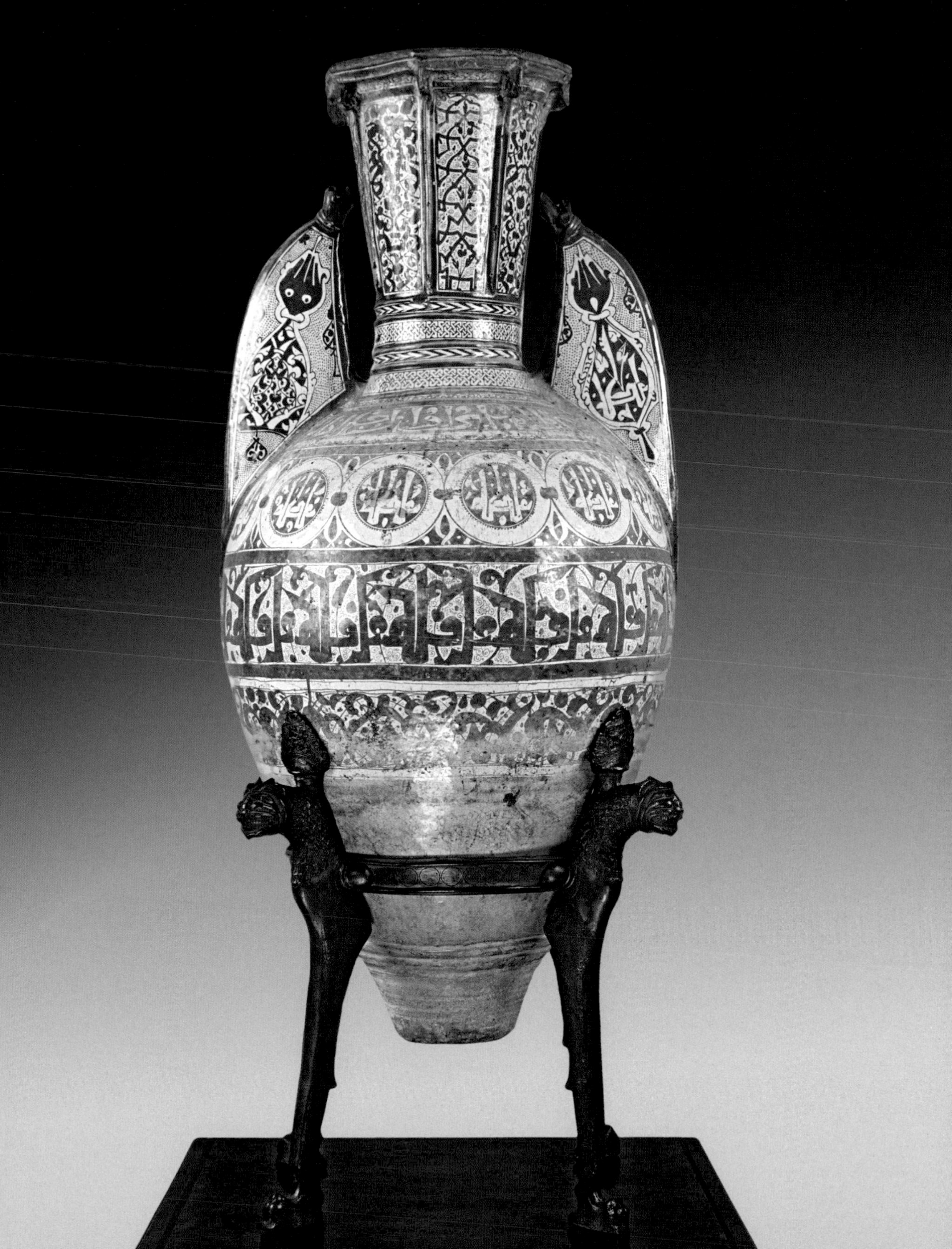

Bowl

Iran (Kashan), ceramic, white glaze, painted with wafer-thin shiny metallic layers on a luster glaze, diameter 35.2 cm, height 3,7 cm
Washington, DC, Freer Gallery of Art

This bowl was made for a cultivated courtier – as is revealed by its lavish use of luster technique (compared with gold) and its ornamentation.

The Arabic inscription on the upper edge contains good wishes for the owner of this piece, characterized as an Emir, great marshal, and warrior. Unfortunately, the name of this Prince is no longer preserved in the text, but the artist is mentioned by name together with the bowl's date of origin. On the side there are other inscriptions of which only fragments have survived. It seems that these are probably verses from popular Persian poems.

At the centre of the bowl's ornamentation is a splendidly bridled horse. Behind this are the heads of five men in courtiers' clothing, and at the animal's feet a groom who has fallen asleep. The lower part of the visual field is filled with water containing fish and a naked female sea-creature. The young groom's face is turned towards the water as if he is dreaming of the beautiful water-sprite. The two different realms depicted are thus linked, producing a unified overall composition otherwise unknown in mediaeval Islamic ceramics.

This unusual scene has repeatedly attracted investigation and interpretation – in particular by Grace Guest and Richard Ettinghausen in 1961. They believe that this scene presents a motif from the repertoire of courtly themes employed from the 12th to the 14th century for ornamentation of all kinds of art objects. However, the fact that the image of an adorned horse is otherwise always shown in conjunction with representation of an enthroned ruler, provokes the assumption that in this case, too, there was also a counterpart, showing a monarch on his throne. Perhaps the bowl was even part of a larger ensemble or service.

The presumption that the painter is illustrating a specific episode from Persian poetry cannot be upheld since the differences from any known texts are too great. Nevertheless, it is possible that interpretation as a courtly motif can be complemented by a second level of significance, taken from the realm of mysticism. Then the scene would be a symbolic depiction of the mystic renouncing rationality (embodied by the horse) and entering into dreamlike contemplation (expressed by the groom's sleep) revealing the beauty of God. In poetry, water is often used as an image of mercy and the Holy Spirit, and it is there that the fish – symbolizing the mystic – lives. Nonetheless it cannot be proved that such an interpretation was intended by either Shamsuddin al-Hasani Abu Zayd or the man who commissioned this bowl.

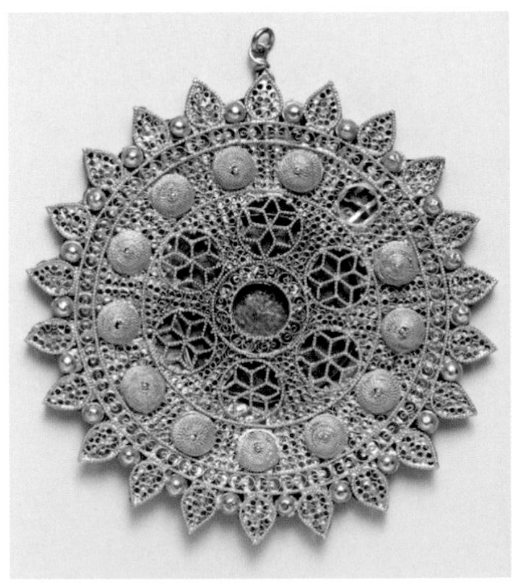

Medallion, Iran, 11th century

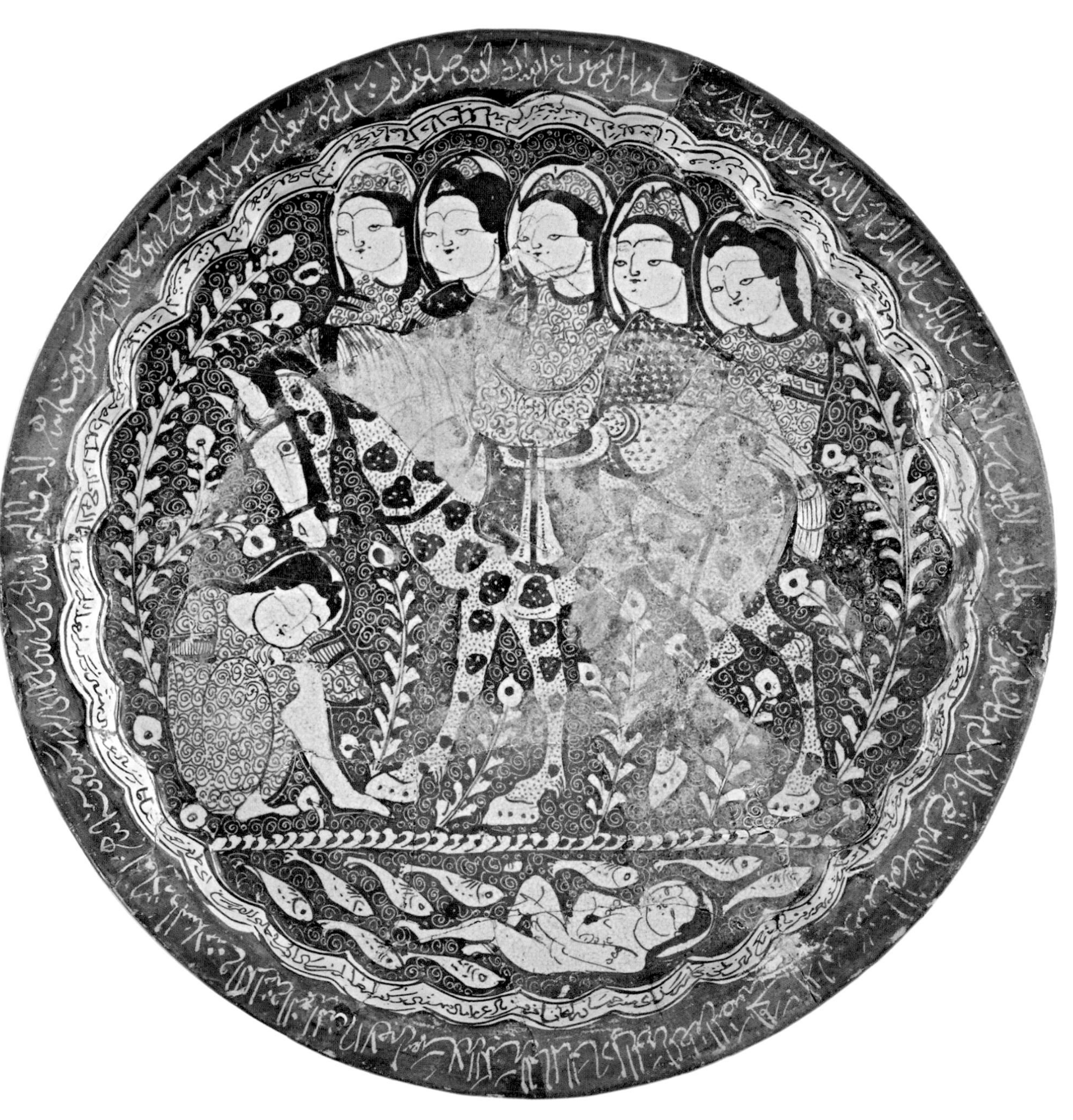

Jonah and the whale

Iran (Tabriz), opaque watercolors, ink, gold on paper, miniature 13 x 26 cm, manuscript 42 x 32 cm
Edinburgh, University Library

The manuscript from which this miniature comes contains an overview of the history of the world from its mythical beginnings until the 14th century. It was commissioned by Rashid al-Din (1247–1318), a Tabriz Vizier who was born Jewish but converted to Islam in 1277. The text and illustrations are based on precursors from a great diversity of periods and cultural backgrounds. Shown here is an episode from the story of the Prophet Jonah, told in the Qur'an (Sura 37, 139–145) and, in considerably more detail, in the Old Testament (Jonah 2, 1–11). Jonah attempts to escape from his calling as a prophet. When a great storm breaks out the ship's crew recognizes – and so does Jonah himself – that he has provoked God's wrath. According to the Qur'an he gambles with his fate, is damned, and thrown into the sea. In the Old Testament he sacrifices himself voluntarily so as to calm the sea and is swallowed by a large fish. In the Bible he now promises to fulfill God's will, and in the Qur'an he is said to praise Allah whereupon the fish vomits him up onto a desolate beach. Here Jonah can only survive because God makes a gourd grow, providing shade.

The miniature shows the situation after Jonah has escaped out of the fish's jaws. On the left the emaciated prophet can be seen seeking protection under the leaves of a bush. On the right is a large carp-like fish whose violent movements churn up the sea. Its scaly body and fins are depicted with great accuracy and vividness. The gourd plant is also represented in great botanical detail in the style of 13th-century scientific miniatures from Mesopotamia (see ill. p. 21 right). The painter has also given the bush fruit so that it can be clearly identified.

This work was produced at a time viewed as the experimental period of Iranian miniature painting. Under the Il-Khan Dynasty, scholars and painters made use of a great variety of models: pre-Islamic texts from Persia and Arabia, Byzantine religious and historical manuscripts, Chinese paintings and woodcuts, and even Western depictions. With the story of Jonah, which had already been shown on sarcophagi from Late Antiquity and in Early Christian and Byzantine art, the artist had an abundance of stimuli at his disposal. Depiction of the gourd plant and of the prophet thus followed Western models, while the carp is reminiscent of Chinese art. The way in which the stormy sea is represented also takes up various traditions. The ornamental and patterned background to the swimming fish follows Arab depictions, and the delicate striated pattern at the edge of the sea adapts Chinese motifs. However, the artist succeeds in creating a new and unified visual form despite these very diverse sources.

"We cast him upon the wilderness, and he was sick, and we caused to grow over him a tree of gourds. Then we sent unto him a hundred thousand or more, and they believed; so we gave them enjoyment for a while."

Qur'an, Sura 37, verses 145–148

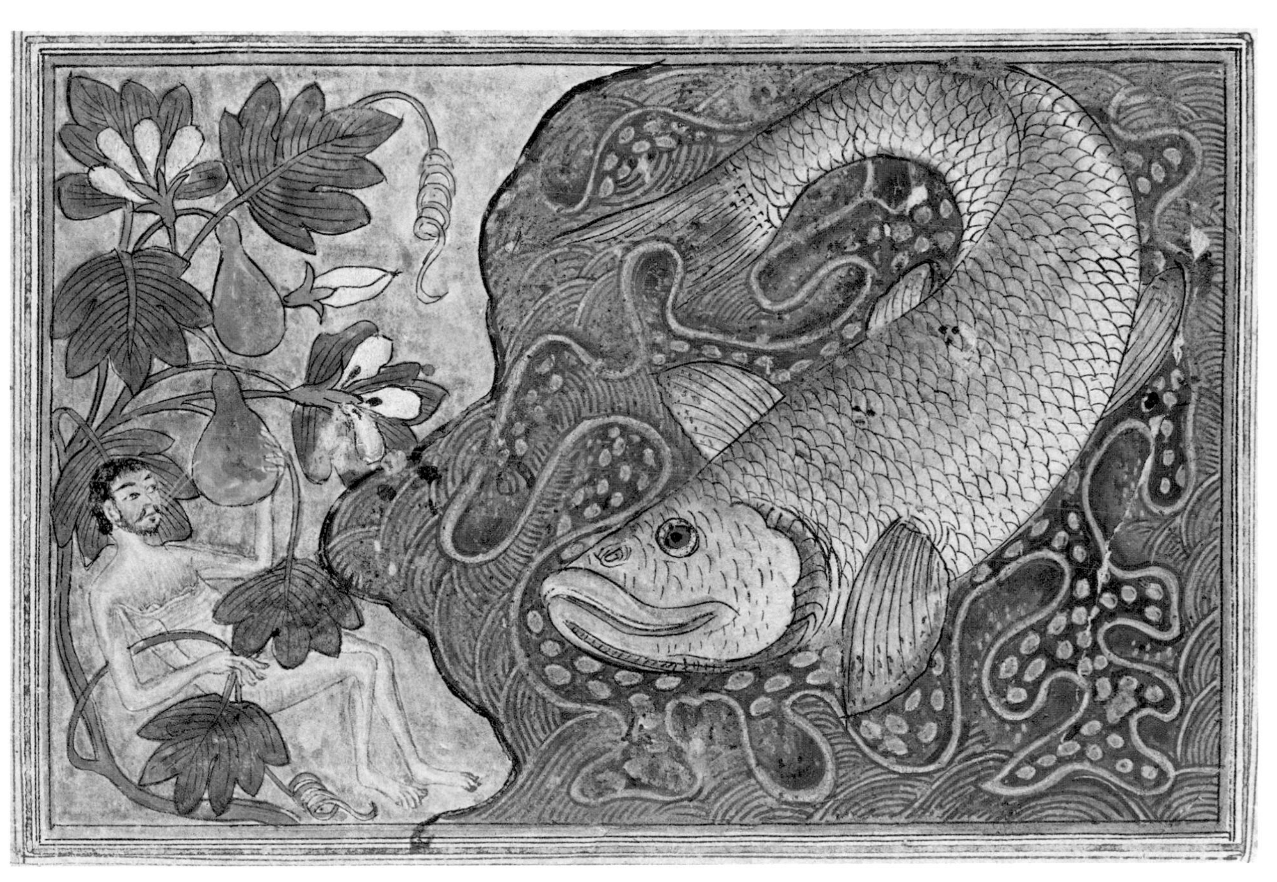

The Archangel Israfil

Probably Iraq, opaque watercolors, ink and gold on paper, 32.7. x 22.4 cm (detail)
Washington, DC, Freer Gallery of Art

In his *Aja'ib al-Makhluqat* ("The Miracle of Creation") Zakariya ibn Muhammad al-Qazwini (1203–1283) describes the dwellers of Earth and Heaven. It is said of the Archangel Israfil that he is the most beautiful of all angels and has four wings: two that separate East and West, one that covers his body, and a fourth that protects his face from God's gaze. Israfil and three other Archangels support God's throne. He blows the breath of life into human beings and also has the task of announcing the Last Judgment with his trumpet. That moment is shown in this miniature from a 14th-century Qazwini manuscript. The Angel has put the trumpet to his lips and strides forcefully forwards. In its style this miniature links elements from Arab painting with Central Asian and Chinese art the influence of which in Iraq began after the conquest of Baghdad in 1258 by Great Khan Hulagu (1256–1265). The figure of the Angel is in general relatively two-dimensional in accordance with Arab-Iraqi tradition. The bold coloring of the wings and clothing is also traditional. Israfil wears a turban, an under-garment with long sleeves, a shorter, closely fitting over-garment with several scarves and sashes, and boots. The folds, most prominent in the under-garment and sashes, are shown in a linear style reminiscent of Central Asian or Chinese depictions. The endings of the sashes, scarves, and belt are highly stylized so that they seem almost ornamental. The orange-green belt terminates in gathered folds, which are also reminiscent of oriental models. The same is true of the motif of the coiled, dragon-like animal head with open jaws at the lower tip of Israfil's wings. Overall, this representation is extremely impressive, particularly because of the Angel's striding movement with the axes pointing in all directions.

In 1922 Ernst Kühnel (1882–1964) included this miniature in his book *Miniature Painting in the Orient*, intensifying the interest of painter Johannes Itten (1888–1967), then working at the Weimar Bauhaus, in Persian book-painting. Four years later Itten drew the Archangel in his diary and wrote: "In this Persian miniature it is mainly the sash swinging far to the front, the line between the left foot and the hands, and the extending beyond the frame that spark off a feeling of movement. It is not sufficient for the subject to suggest movement illustratively; movement must be generated by displacements of balance, multiplicity, and turbulent lines." Itten also studied the "directional contrast" he observed in other oriental miniatures and compared these with European depictions from different times. With such "structural analyses" he wanted to develop in his students a genuine understanding of painting through it's underlying principles.

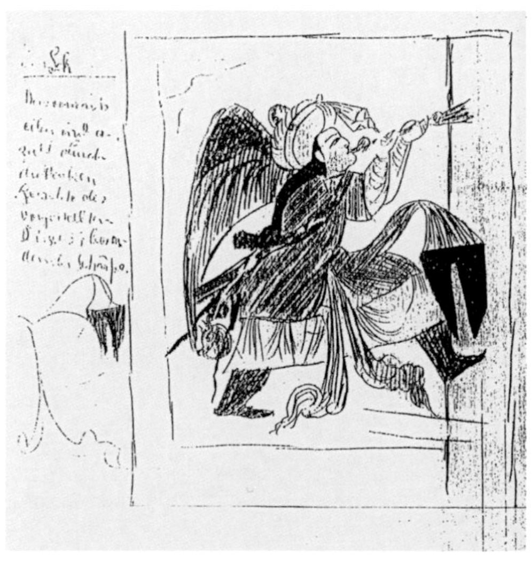

Johannes Itten, The Archangel Israfil, drawing in a diary, Germany (Berlin), 1926

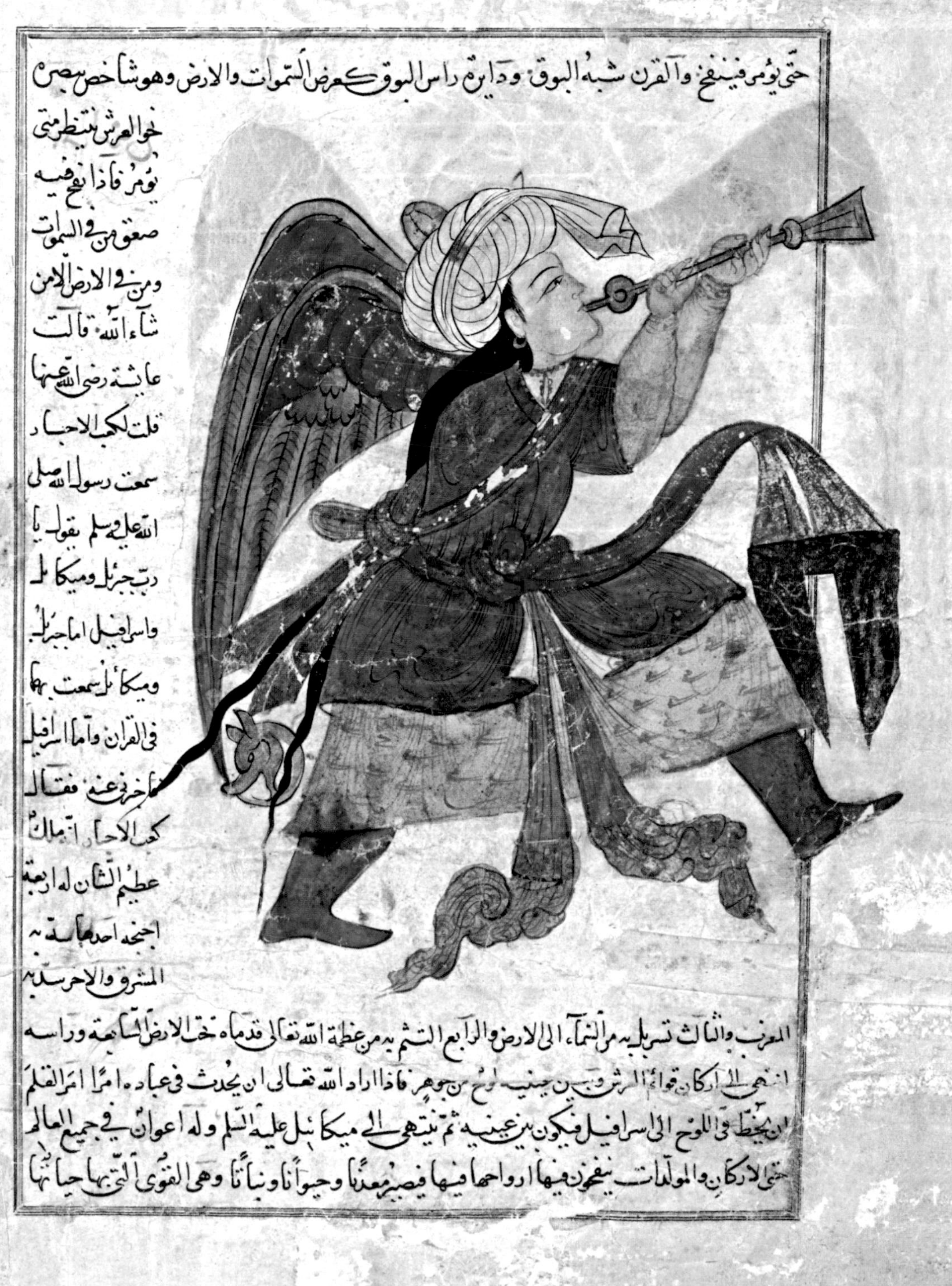
حتى يؤمر فينفخ والقرن شبه البوق ودايرة راس البوق كعرض السموات والارض وهو شاخص بصره
نحو العرش ينتظر متى
يؤمر فاذا نفخ فيه
صعق من في السموات
ومن في الارض الا من
شاء الله قالت
عايشة رضي الله عنها
قلت لكعب الاحبار
سمعت رسول الله صلى
الله عليه وسلم يقول يا
رب جبرئيل وميكائيل
واسرافيل اما جبرئيل
وميكائيل سمعت بهما
في القران واما اسرافيل
فاخبرني عنه فقال
كعب الاحبار انه ملك
عظيم الشان له اربعة
اجنحة احدها سد به
المشرق والاخر سد به
المغرب والثالث تسربل به من السماء الى الارض والرابع التثم به من عظمة الله تعالى قدماه تحت الارض السابعة وراسه
انتهى الى اركان قوائم العرش وبين عينيه لوح من جوهر فاذا اراد الله تعالى ان يحدث في عباده امرا امر القلم
ان يخط في اللوح الى اسرافيل فيكون بين عينيه ثم ينتهي الى ميكائيل عليه السلم وله اعوان في جميع العالم
حتى الاركان والمولدات ينفخون فيها ارواحها فيصير معدنا وحيوانا ونباتا وهي القوى التي بها حياتها

TWO Eagles

Iran, ink, opaque watercolors, gold on paper, miniature 14.6 x 15.7 cm, entire page 40.3 x 31.8 cm (detail)
New York, NY, The Metropolitan Museum of Art

This picture of a pair of eagles comes from a now scattered manuscript of the *Kitab Na't al-Hayawan wa-Manafi' ihi* ("Book on the Identification and Utilization of Animals") written by ibn Bakhtishu. The author, who came from a long-established and esteemed family of Nestorian Greek doctors, wrote his work in 941 for Caliph al-Muttaqi (934–944), whose personal physician he was. The earliest surviving manuscript of this text was produced around 1220 in Mosul, and the first version in Persian was probably made in 1298 at Maragha (110 km south of Tabriz) during the time of Ilkhanid ruler Mahmud Ghazan Khan (1295–1304). Today the manuscript is at the Pierpont Morgan Library in New York. It may have served as a model for what is shown here, since its illustrations are very similar to those which can be attributed to the scattered manuscript.

The style of this miniature indicates that it was painted at the start of the 14th century during a period, when artists in Persia's court workshops frequently used older manuscripts as models and processed a great variety of influences in their creations. It is clearly apparent in this picture of a pair of eagles that older Mesopotamian depictions have been studied and that inspiration also came from East-Asian art. The generally two-dimensional representation of the birds' bodies, the way they are resting, and the larger-than-life stylized plants were taken over from 13th century Arab painting. It is useful to compare them with the Hariri manuscripts (ill. p. 37) and scientific texts (see ills p. 12 left, 21 right). The same applies to the greatly reduced landscape on the lower edge of the picture and its compositional counterpart: an abstract segment of sky with a sun, red stars, and clouds.

On the other hand, the way in which individual details in the picture are portrayed follows models from Chinese art in the 10th to13th century. That is the case in the shape of the clouds and in the large lotus and peony blossoms alongside and between the two birds. The miniature's restrained use of color also derives from Chinese influences. Persian artists probably gained extensive knowledge of Chinese art from craft objects (painted porcelain, textiles, and silk embroidery) exported to the West. However these models were not simply copied; they served painters in Iran as a starting-point for new creations of their own, as the comparison of the flying eagle in this miniature with a Chinese example makes clear (ill. p. 52). In the Persian painting the bird is made more strongly two-dimensional. In addition, accentuation of individual lines on the neck and wings to some extent introduces a calligraphic element, which the Chinese representation does not possess, despite all the similarities of motif.

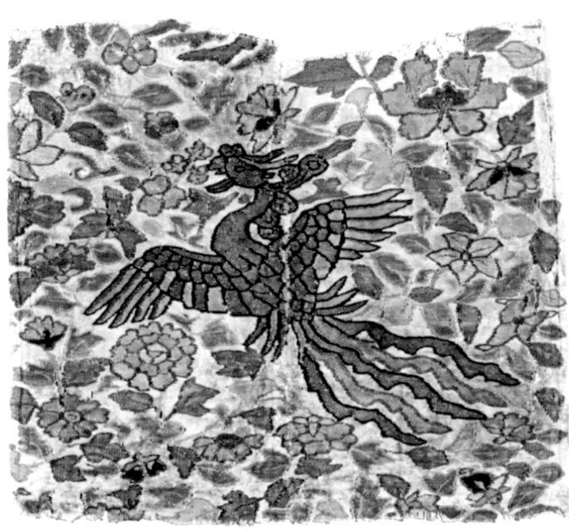

Phoenix Among Flowers, China, Northern Song Dynasty, 10th–12th century

اگه کسی و دمزو ن بر خایه نشنبید و از مرغان هر ایج کبران تر باشد بچه بن و مهر ابچه مبا ند نز

ببینت و دو روز و ا اله ببیانی سه خایه نهد و سه بچه بر ارد و یکی را بیندازد و مرغی بیت

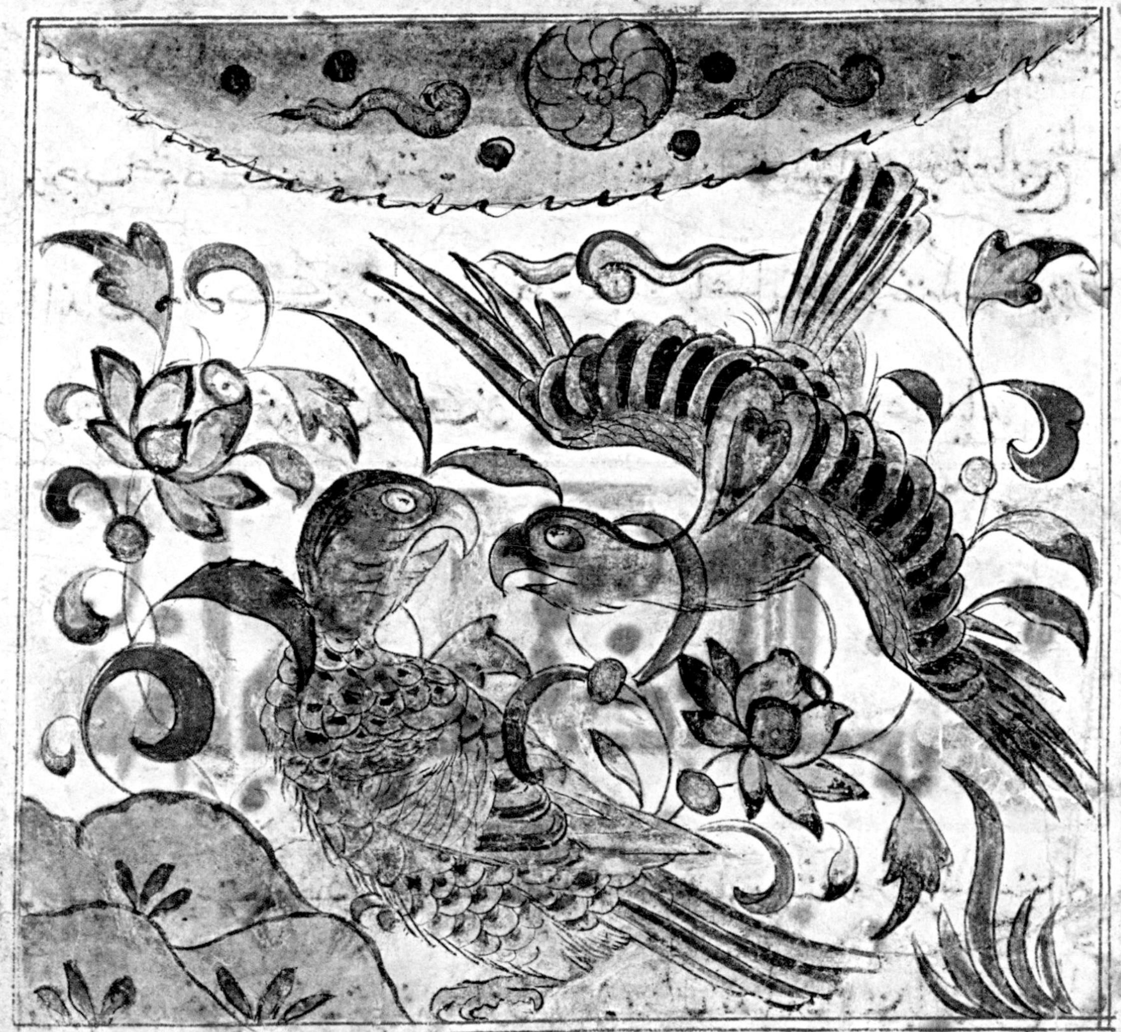

استخوان شکن او را بر دارد و برد آ که چون او بپر شد و ... و نتواند ...

لحکان او را بر دارند و منزل منزل می برند و تا افتاب برنیابد از جای خویش نجنبد

River Landscape with Trees

Iran, drawing, ink and opaque watercolors on paper, 20.4 x 29 cm (detail)
Berlin, Staatsbibliothek, Oriental Department

Depictions devoted solely to landscape are extremely rare in mediaeval Islamic painting. There, landscape motifs usually appear as a complement to or background for set-pieces or human figures. A few 14th century manuscripts, produced at Tabriz for people close to art patron Vizier Rashid al-Din (1247–1318), constitute an exception. There are some paintings devoted solely to landscapes in the *Jami al-Tawarikh* ("World Chronicle") he assembled. The work here, today included in an album of collected oriental miniatures, may well originally have come from a *Jami al-Tawarikh* manuscript – as is shown by comparison with other representations still preserved in their original state.

Tabriz artists strikingly often resorted to Chinese models in their creation of landscapes – to scrolled pictures of the 7th to the 13th century, woodcuts, miniatures, and also depictions on porcelain. Eastern influences are also clearly visible in the representation here of a river and its tree-lined banks. The twisted forms of the bare, gnarled trees derive from Chinese models as well, and so do the absolutely regular shapes of the waves and their foaming crests.

The painter constructed the overall landscape in diagonal bands. The bushes in the foreground and the slight bend in the river enabled him to create the impression of a degree of spatial depth. He deliberately chose his format so that the picture's frame intersects the net-like branches of the trees along the upper edge, and the entire depiction thus appears like a natural distillation from what in reality is a much larger landscape.

The great quality of this composition becomes clear in comparison with a landscape in another Tabriz manuscript. This, too, presents a river, this time flowing through high rocks covered with trees. However, here the construction of the landscape is much more conventional, since the water flows almost parallel to the lower edge of the depiction and the rocks rise up parallel to the picture's surface. On the other hand, the artist also strove to enliven his representation. Many fish and a couple of ducks are to be seen in the river, and the size and shape of trees are extremely diverse. Depiction of the strange rocks and the water are also influenced by Chinese miniatures. The artists apparently knew the illustrations in late 13th century Arab manuscripts. Both of these depictions show what skills artists possessed in early 14th century workshops. They united a wide range of ideas in convincing compositions and included details that were no longer taken into account in later Persian painting.

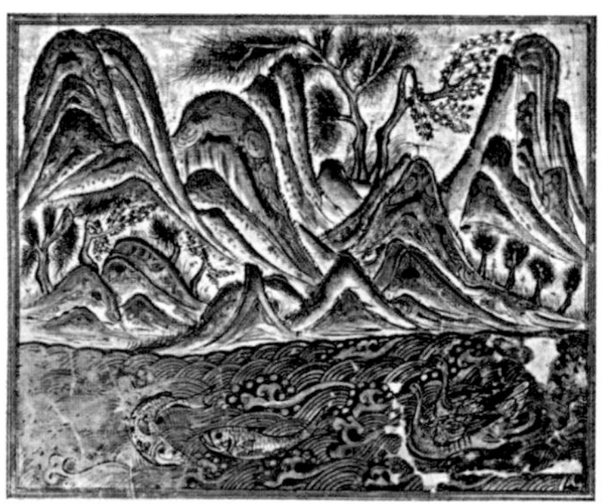

Unknown Painter from Tabriz, The Mountains of India, Iran (Tabriz, Rashidya District), 1314

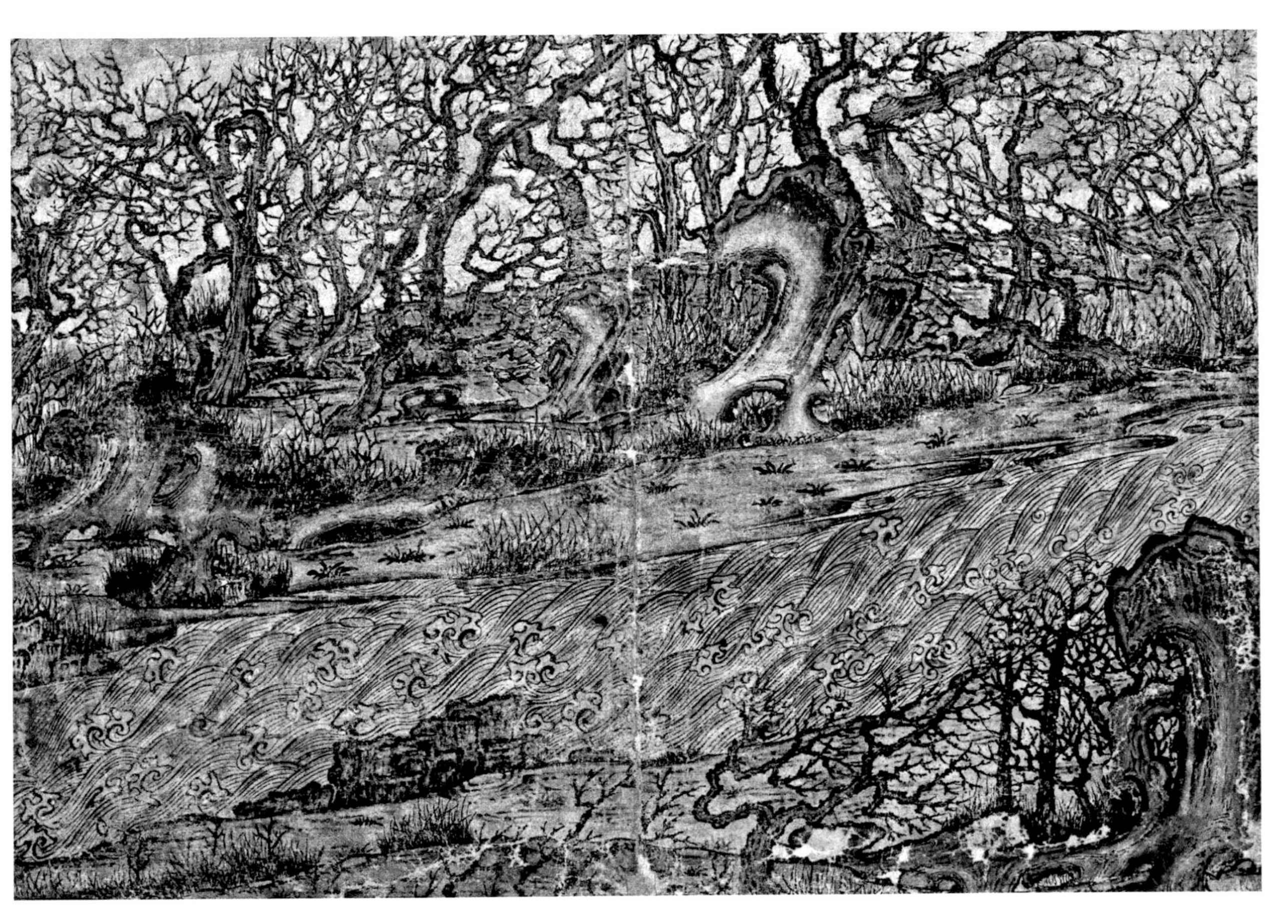

Isfandiar's struggle with the simurgh

Iran (Shiraz), opaque watercolors, ink on paper, miniature 12 x 22.5 cm
Istanbul, Topkapi Palace Museum

Isfandiar is one of Iran's mythical heroes. According to legend, he was invulnerable. Stories about his deeds were collected, together with traditions about the lives of pre-Islamic Persian rulers, by Firdawsi (940/941–1020), the poet from Tus, in an epic almost 50,000 verses long. Today the *Shahnama* ("Book of Kings") is still seen as Iran's greatest literary legacy. 14th century *Shahnama* manuscripts are historically important because no earlier illustrated copies of this work have been found up to the present day. Comparable scenes are only known from earlier ceramics and metalwork (see ills p. 11 and 30). These images on works of applied art show that even before the surviving book-illustrations Firdawsi's "Book of Kings" inspired artists and gave rise to a Persian school of painting. In addition, sources from the 10th to the 12th century report that painted castle walls in Iran and Mesopotamia were also influenced by the Sassanid period. It can thus be assumed that similar representations already existed in contemporary book-painting. These connections demonstrate the importance of a pre-Islamic culture of narrative for the development of Persian painting from the 13th century. These artistic references to earlier models were deliberate, so that development can be called a renaissance.

In Firdawsi, the simurgh ("30 birds") appears in two forms, and both aspects are mixed. It was originally known to Iranian mythology as a bountiful female hybrid with a dog's head, lion's paws, and a peacock's tail. During the Islamic epoch this fabulous creature was presented as a huge magical bird with the head of a predator and two horns. One of Isfandiar's heroic deeds entailed killing this malign simurgh.

In this small miniature Isfandiar is to be seen on the left of the picture as he kills the magical bird. This scene is set in the mountains where the simurgh lives. Isfandiar has raised his shield on high with one hand, and deals a deadly blow to the simurgh with the sword held in the other – his left hand. This depiction is reduced to essentials with the significance of this victory over the all-powerful bird, further emphasized by the latter taking up two-thirds of the picture with its feathers, which will be scattered all over the world, extending beyond the frame. The text mentions that Isfandiar set off for this confrontation in a chariot. Only its two wheels beneath the bird's body reveal this vehicle.

The resplendent magical bird is the dominant element in this miniature. Its posture and abundant tail-feathers are based on Chinese depictions of the phoenix, and being the Empress' emblem was thus a symbol of femininity. This bird is presented with sharp talons, a highly mobile, shifting body, and splendid feathers, fitting it for appropriation of and transformation into the magical creature from the *Shahnama*.

"Thou must hold thine own against the simurgh, the princess of birds as high as a mountain and wilder than lions and elephants. When her wings sweep across the earth, the land quakes and the skies become dark."

Firdawsi, Shahnama ("Book of Kings"), 1020

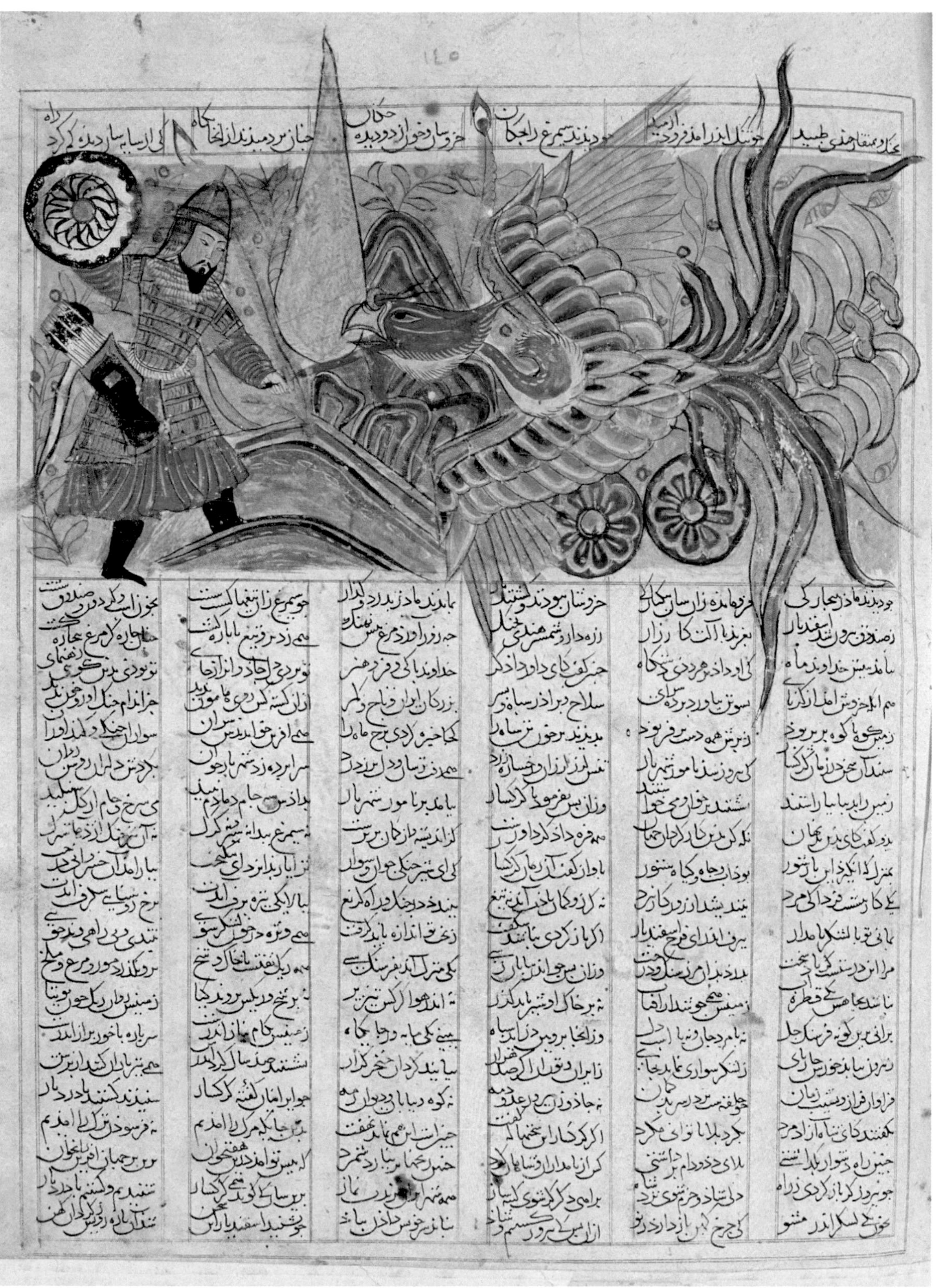

UNKNOWN PERSIAN PAINTER, PROBABLY ACTIVE IN TABRIZ c. 1335/1336

Lamenting the Dead Alexander

Iran (Tabriz), ink, opaque watercolors, gold on paper, 57.6 x 39.7 cm
Washington, DC, Freer Gallery of Art

This miniature comes from a now scattered manuscript of Firdawsi's (940/941–1020) *Shahnama*, viewed as a masterpiece of 14th century Iranian painting. During political upheavals in Iran (1905/1906–1909), what was known as the "Great Mongolian *Shahnama*" came into the hands of Georges Demotte, a Parisian art-dealer (1877–1923), who took this apart and sold individual pages containing miniatures. Today only 58 miniatures remain of the original 280 pages and 190 pictures. Firdawsi's text recounts the history of Persian rulers from their mythical beginnings to the Middle Ages and includes the life of Alexander the Great (356–323 BC), the Greek conqueror who was originally to be seen in 12 of this manuscript's illustrations. The miniature shown here depicts the lying-in-state of the King and the accompanying lamentations. At the centre of the picture is Alexander's coffin, onto which the dead man's mother has thrown herself in a dramatic pose. Opposite her is Alexander's teacher, the philosopher Aristotle (384–322 BC), who is holding a handkerchief to his mouth and weeping. Standing around the two main figures are groups of sorrowful courtiers. At the front edge of the miniature lamenting women kneel, tearing their hair.

The central event is placed in a special architectural setting. The observer's gaze is directed towards the main scene. That effect is strengthened by curtains drawn to the side, creating the impression of a stage. The contrast between the colors of blue-grey, red, and gold determines the impact of this dramatic scene of mourning. Analysis of compositional relationships in this scene reveals a well thought-through use of space and color, and also clarifies details inspired by a range of models. The architectural frame and the art objects mentioned are extremely accurate in their reflection of real Iranian artifacts, while the perspective indicated and the depiction of robes and folds are influenced by Byzantine painting. On the other hand, some faces and figures are reminiscent of Central or East Asian representations.

The various craft objects used as furnishings accord with surviving examples from the 14th century: four large brass candelabra, hanging lamps of enameled glass, and an incense container above the bier. The floor is covered with carpets, as also documented on other miniatures. Such rich provision for the lamentation of Alexander absolutely follows Firdawsi's description of this episode. He reports that the ruler's coffin was set up in Iskandria (i.e. Babylon) where over 100,000 mourners defiled past the grave. Firdawsi also describes the despair of Alexander's mother, who – as the miniature shows – pressed her face against the dead man's body. It was not often that Persian painting so expressively and successfully represented the feeling of mourning as in this depiction.

"when my musk throne crumbles into dust while the pure soul floats up to the realm of the blessed, do not wear sackcloth and ashes. No, rather moisten your tongues in order to forgive me."

Nizami, The Book of Alexander, c. 1204

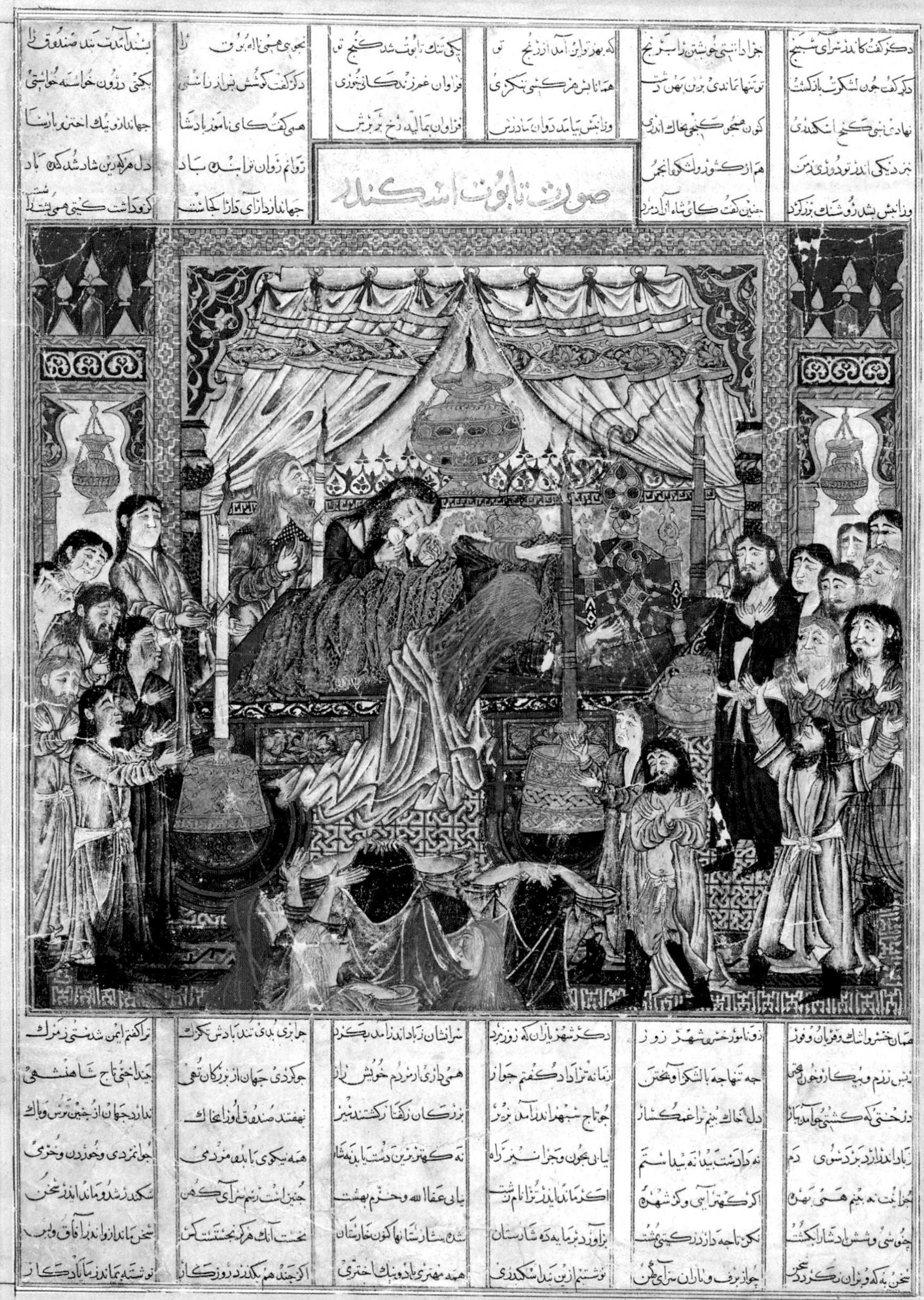
صورت تابوت اسکندر

The Owl and the Raven

Afghanistan (Herat), opaque watercolors, ink, gold on paper, 28.7 x 19.7 cm (detail)
Istanbul, Topkapi Palace Museum

Prince Baisunghur Mirza (d. 1433), the son of Timurid ruler, Shah Rukh (1405–1447), had a particular liking for *Kalila wa Dimna* ("Kalila and Dimna"). He had two manuscripts made of this text, and the one selected here is among the Herat school's most outstanding creations.

Kalila wa Dimna was a manual for royal sons the stories of which were intended to provide an entertaining way of making Princes into just, diplomatic, and wise men. At the start of each chapter a King asks a philosopher about the consequences of individual actions, and the philosopher explains these by way of moralizing stories, where animals play the main role.

These stories originally go back to Bidpai (3rd century AD), an Indian sage, and are therefore also known as the "Fables of Bidpai". They were widely disseminated as the *Panchatantra* ("Five Principles") and translated into Middle Persian as early as c. 550, into Arabic around 750, and into New Persian in the 12th century. A Latin translation in the 13th century influenced European literature, and Oriental influences are apparent in the Fables of Jean de La Fontaine (1621–1695) and in Johann Wolfgang von Goethe's (1749–1832) *Reineke Fuchs*.

The miniature selected here shows an episode from the story of a dispute between owls and ravens. One night the owls attacked the ravens and killed many of them. One of the survivors was questioned by the King of the Owls so as to settle the dispute. His cleverness allows the ravens to take their revenge and to smoke the owls out of their mountain caves.

The manuscript page is divided in two. Above is a framed and isolated block of text, and below that the miniature. On the right side and below, the framing of the text is also continued around the image. It is absent on the left so that here the painting can develop beyond the limits of the text.

In the foreground of this miniature stands the raven's delegate on a meadow mounting diagonally to the right. He is talking with the owls who are sitting on bizarrely shaped rocks. Behind them can be seen a meadow extending to the upper edge of the picture. A profusely flowering tree terminates the picture on the left, establishing a particular emphasis within the landscape. The group of eight owls appears calm and united despite the diversity of head movements. While the King and the two birds next to him look directly at the raven standing in front of them, the other owls behind are looking to the left. The painter thus draws the observer's attention to the tree and the raven, which are compositionally related and emphasized through their dark coloring. Stylistically, the miniature follows the early 14th century Herat school of painting in its processing of models from East Asian art (see ills p. 53, 54, 55) and 13th century Mesopotamian painting (see ills p. 21, 37). Those different influences are also recognizable here: in the shaping of the rocks and in the stylized flowers and plants. In addition, a particular color-palette, emphasizing mauve, turquoise, and a radiant dark-blue, is characteristic of this manuscript.

"Thine eye may sleep but what weighs on the mind awakens and curses thee – and Allah's eye does not slumber."

1001 Nights, Story of the Wolf and the Fox

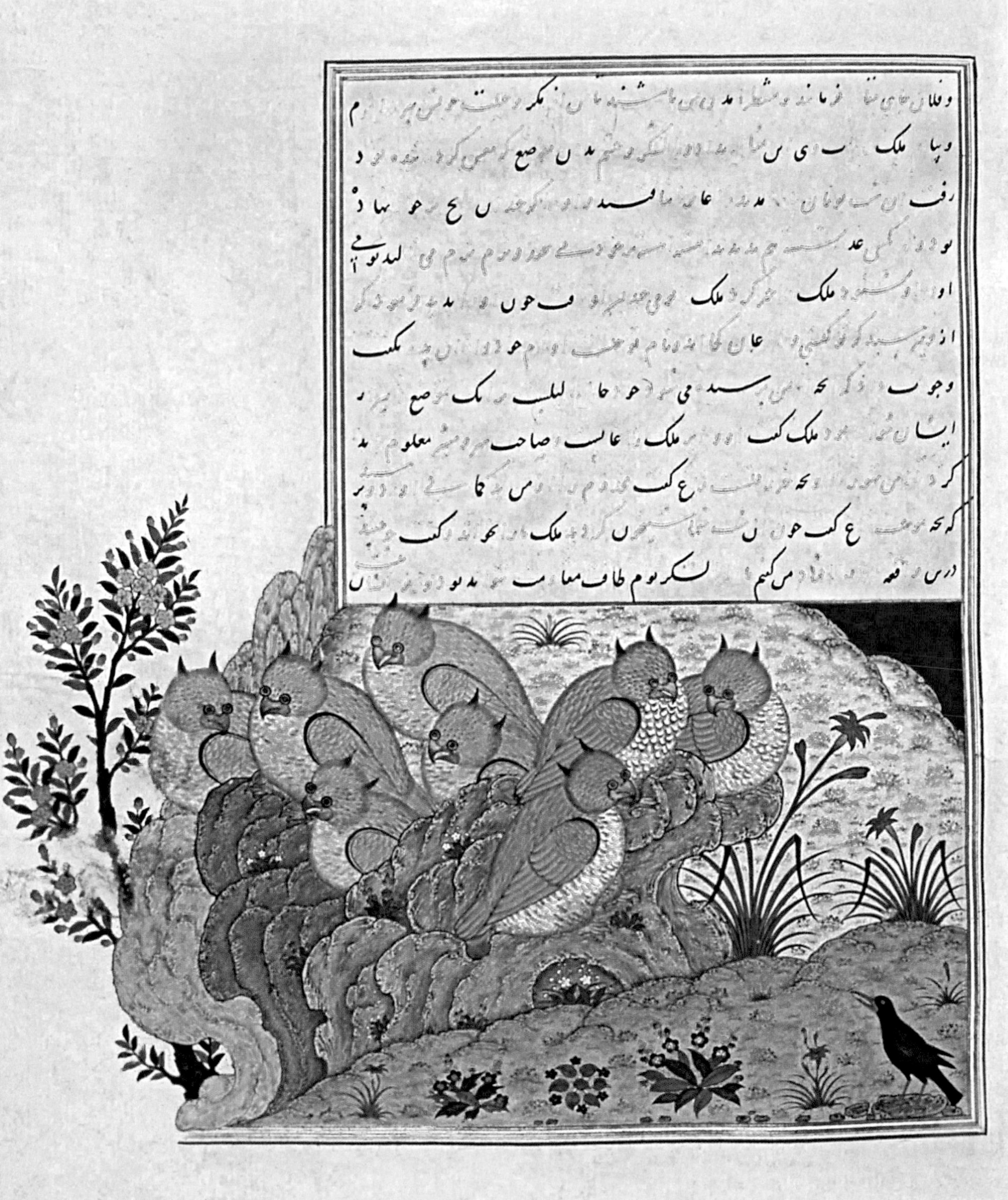

The Prophet Muhammad Before David and Solomon

Afghanistan (Herat), opaque watercolors, gold, silver on paper, entire page 34.3 x 25.4 cm
Paris, Bibliothèque nationale de France

This *Mirajnama* ("History of the Ascent to Heaven"), describing the Prophet Muhammad's journey, is another of the manuscripts produced in Herat at the beginning of the 15th century during the reign of Shah Rukh (1405–1447) – see also ill. p. 61. The manuscript includes 63 unique miniatures revealing Central Asian Buddhist influences, but is nevertheless attributable to Herat through comparing styles. The text was translated by Mir Haydar from the Arabic original into East Turkish and the manuscript is written in Uiguric (the language of an Islamic Turkic people in China) with headings in Arabic, Turkish, and Persian. The calligrapher was Malik Bakhshi.

In 1673 the book was bought in Istanbul by Antoine Galland (1646–1715), the French Orientalist and first European translator of *The Thousand and One Nights*. Muhammad's flight across the heavens was a popular theme in Islamic miniature painting, but usually only the journey itself is depicted. It is told that in a single night Muhammad rode across the skies from Mecca to Jerusalem and back again. This visionary traversing of the heavens was seen as a sign of God's blessing, as a token of divine favor towards His Messenger, Muhammad. During this journey through the seven heavens Muhammad experienced particular closeness to God. First he met various prophets (including Adam), who taught him about the religious duties of the faithful, and then finally Muhammad came before God Himself and was instructed in the five obligatory daily prayers. He was accompanied by the Archangel Gabriel, characterized by large multicolored wings and a crown. This miniature shows Muhammad's meeting with two prophets, David and Solomon, in the third heaven. Muhammad appears on the right with his winged horse Buraq, an Islamic mythical creature which only appears in representations of the Prophet's heavenly journey. Buraq is not mentioned in Sura 17 of the Qur'an, describing this ascent, but appears in other literary sources from the 11th century (in miniatures only from the 14th century).

Muhammad's face is freely visible rather than being veiled as in a lot of later manuscripts. As in many other depictions he is wearing a green robe, which is why green is often thought to be the Prophet's color.

The figures float in a starry sky traversed by strips of golden clouds in a very animated Chinese style (see ills p. 7 and p. 65). The twisting of the long belt of Gabriel's robe also spans the heavens. Behind the prophets' heads are haloes of golden flames. Muhammad's halo is particularly large and extends across the entire sky.

This *Mirajnama* characterizes the situation at the Herat court where text and miniatures united Western (Arabic and Persian) traditions with Central Asian and Chinese elements. In the 15th century a great variety of cultural trends intermingled there, giving rise to a new and completely autonomous art.

"He took another step out of his being and became capable of looking at God, truly saw his Lord, and wiped from his eyes everything he had ever seen before."

Nizami, Khamsa ("Five Stories"), 1197

13

رُؤْيَتُهُ صَلَّى ٱللهُ عَلَيْهِ وَسَلَّمَ لِدَاوُودَ وَسُلَيْمَانَ عَلَيْهِمَا ٱلسَّلَامُ

رسول الله صلى الله عليه وسلم داود پيغمبر و سليمان پيغامبر عليهما السلام ايله مصاحبت اتدكاري مقام در

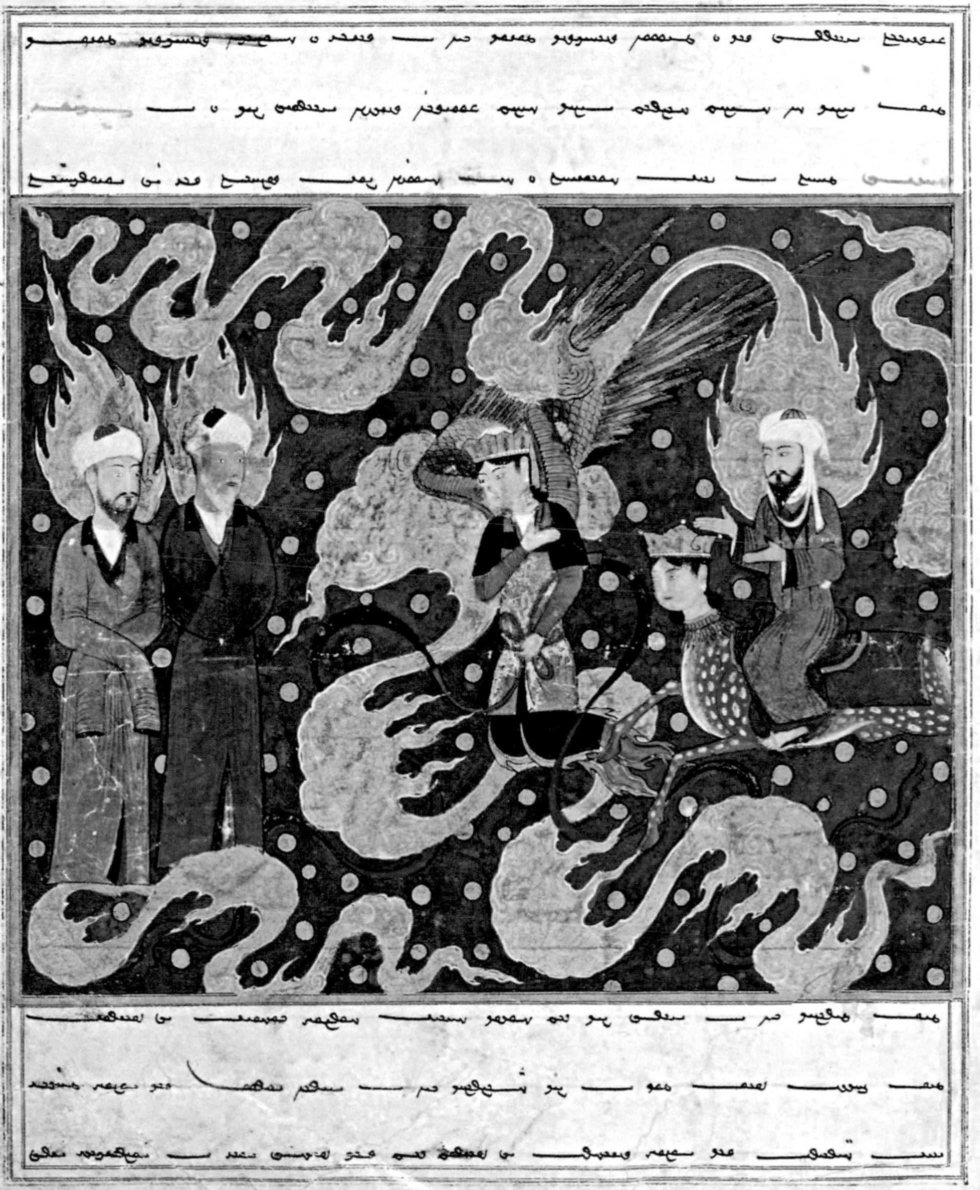

Festivity at a Princely court

Iran (Shiraz), opaque watercolors and gold on paper, right-hand side of a double title-page, 32.5 x 22.1 cm
Cleveland, OH, The Cleveland Museum of Art

In the mid-15th century there was an important artists' workshop at Shiraz. Here the early Timurid style was developed after the city was conquered by the Muzaffarids in 1353. Shiraz was the capital of the Timurid Empire until 1452. Miniatures produced in the court workshop combined aspects of painting from Herat with local characteristics – as becomes clear in depictions of people based on the Shiraz tradition and also in representations of clouds and plants.

This miniature exemplifies the style of the Shiraz workshop. Together with a second sheet (ill. p. 64) it probably constituted the title-page ornamentation of a *Shahnama* ("Book of Kings") manuscript produced under Shah Rukh (1305–1447). Today the main part of this manuscript is in the Bibliothèque nationale in Paris, while individual pages are in other collections.

Both halves of the title-page are linked as a composition. They show a festive scene in an idealized landscape by a river. The size of this area, demonstrated in the upper part of the left-hand sheet (ill. p. 64), shows that this is probably a princely garden. Bushes and trees blossom abundantly, and there are flowers along the banks of the stream. All the blossoms are large and two-dimensional, but highly diverse in form. The sky is indicated by way of strangely shaped clouds the ornamental forms of which reveal East-Asian influences.

Within the garden are a great variety of scenes characteristic of courtly celebrations. On the left (ill. p. 64) groups of courtiers are presented in lively conversation – particularly striking are the two men with polo sticks at the centre of the picture – and on the right is the main group of participants. Here is a canopy made of rich brocade beneath which the royal couple sits. The princess stretches out her right arm to the prince opposite, who wants to hand her a present. The couple is surrounded by many courtiers. The ladies are to the left of the princess, and in the foreground servants are offering food on golden platters and drinks in precious Chinese porcelain vessels. Important guests sit on carpets spread out on the grass (today such carpets are only known from depictions in miniatures). At the lower edge kneel a singer and a musician playing a large harp.

The diversity of arrangement of the different figures and their lively gestures make this a highly vivacious depiction. Above all, this scene emanates harmony and well-being, impressively demonstrating the luxury that really did characterize life at the Timurid courts of Herat and Shiraz. Courtiers possessed the much-admired blue-and-white porcelain from the time of China's Ming Dynasty (1368–1644) and made use of splendid gold and jade objects.

"This picture exemplifies sovereign mastery and subordination of the representational to purely artistic formal rules while fully upholding a truth full of life".

Ernst Diez, The Art of Islamic Peoples, 1915

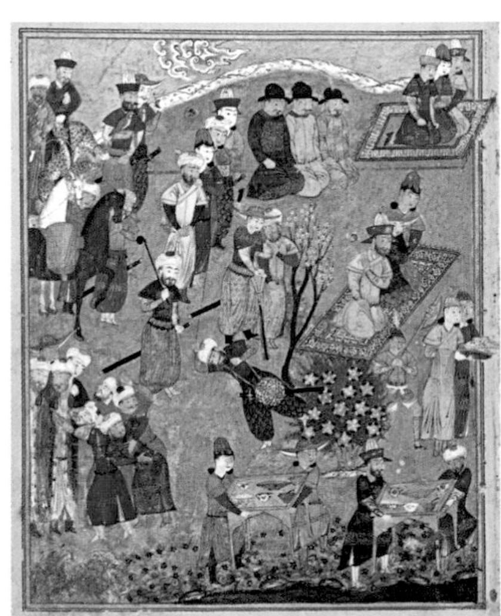

Left-hand side of the title-page

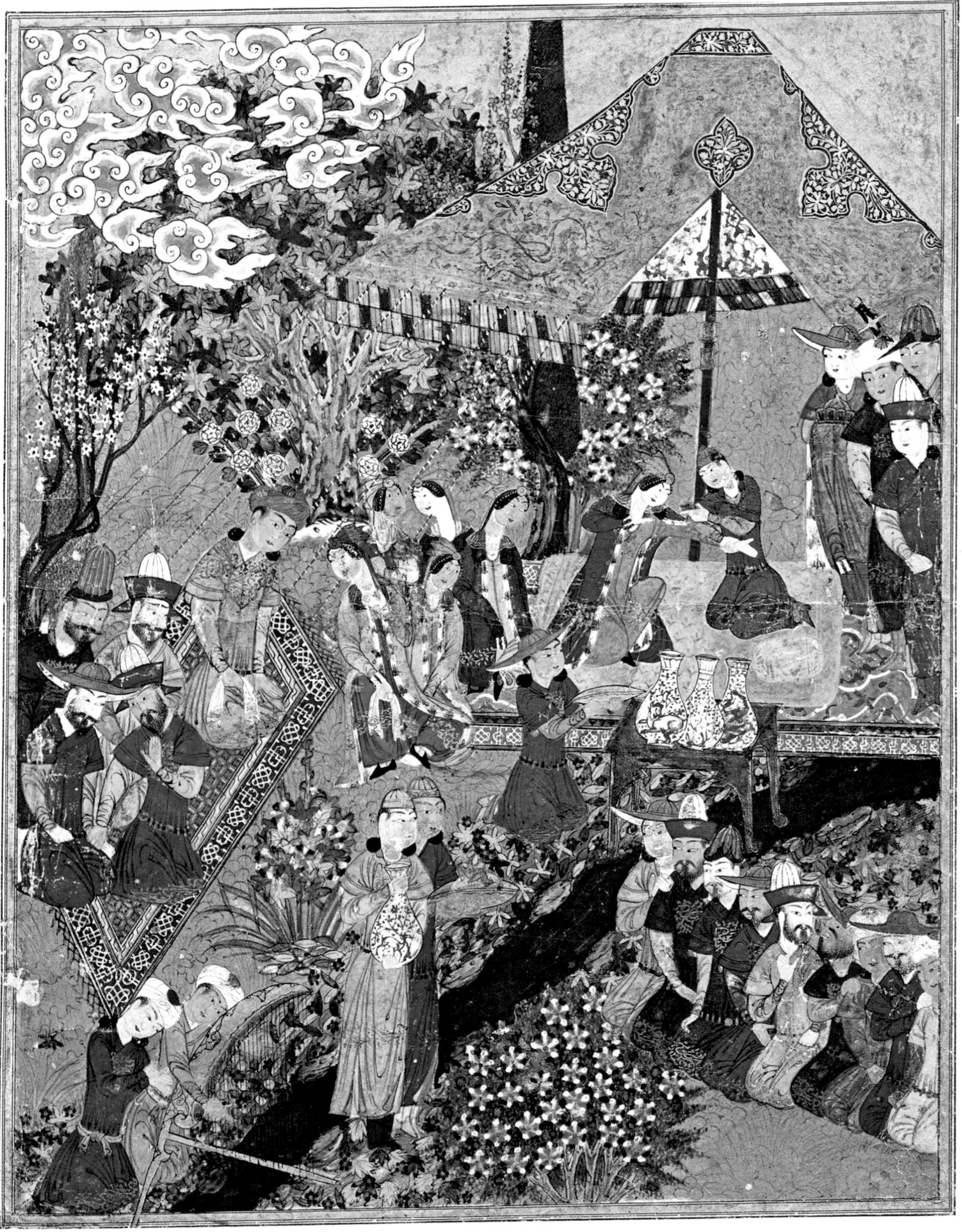

Isfandiar Kills Arjasp in the "Former Palace"

Afghanistan (Herat), opaque watercolors, ink, gold on paper, entire page 38 x 26 cm
Tehran, Gulistan Palace

The *Shahnama* ("Book of Kings") manuscript from which this miniature comes can be seen as *the* masterpiece by artists from the workshop of Prince Baisunghur Mirza (d. 1433). This large manuscript is furnished with a two-sided title-page and 20 miniatures, and bound in precious leather with gilded decoration in relief. The text's writer was Mawlana Ja'far, director of Baisunghur's library, and one of that period's most important calligraphers. Various artists worked on the miniatures. Prince Baisunghur, who commissioned the manuscript, might even have been depicted in a scene from another manuscript (ill. p. 24 right) showing a ruler sitting in a garden.

The miniature selected here presents the battle between two mythological heroes, Isfandiar and Arjasp. The latter, King of Turan, has abducted Isfandiar's sisters and imprisoned them in his place. Disguised as a merchant, Isfandiar succeeds in getting into his presence, killing him after a nocturnal drinking spree. He then liberates his sisters and burns down the palace.

In its upper part the miniature shows the moment when Isfandiar decapitates his enemy. However, the main motif is actually Arjasp's large and splendid "former palace" with its walls, towers, and gateways. The painter clearly based this on the architecture and ornamentation of his time since everything depicted accords with 15th century buildings in Herat, with their strong walls and decorative facades of tiles.

External and inner aspects alternate in the presentation of individual parts of the building. At the bottom of the miniature the surrounding wall and the castle's towers are shown from outside. From the inside you can also see more towers and the little pavilion-like building, where Arjasp's soldiers keep watch over Isfandiar's sisters. Alongside this space are a number of tower-like elements unrelated to the rest of the architecture. Above that there are hints (in a highly reduced form) of a second ring of castle fortifications. This allows a view of the interior of the throne-room, splendidly decorated with tiles, where Isfandiar's armed supporters observe the fight between the two protagonists.

The individual elements in this architecture may be comprehended in perspective, but they lead a life of their own and do not form any logical interconnection. The perspective cannot be related to the building's overall structure, either. However, it is precisely this particularity that makes the miniature so attractive for today's observer; the way different elements in the picture are separated seems very free – almost like modern abstract painting.

The lessons to be learned from the death of Arjasp are summarized in a 1925 translation of the *Shahnama*: "That is the way of the world. First it fills our glass with sweet wine, then it showers us with poisons. Do not attach your heart to this house of transient dealings. Nothing remains whether you are a King or a peasant. Fate determines your path." (Firdawsi, c. 1020).

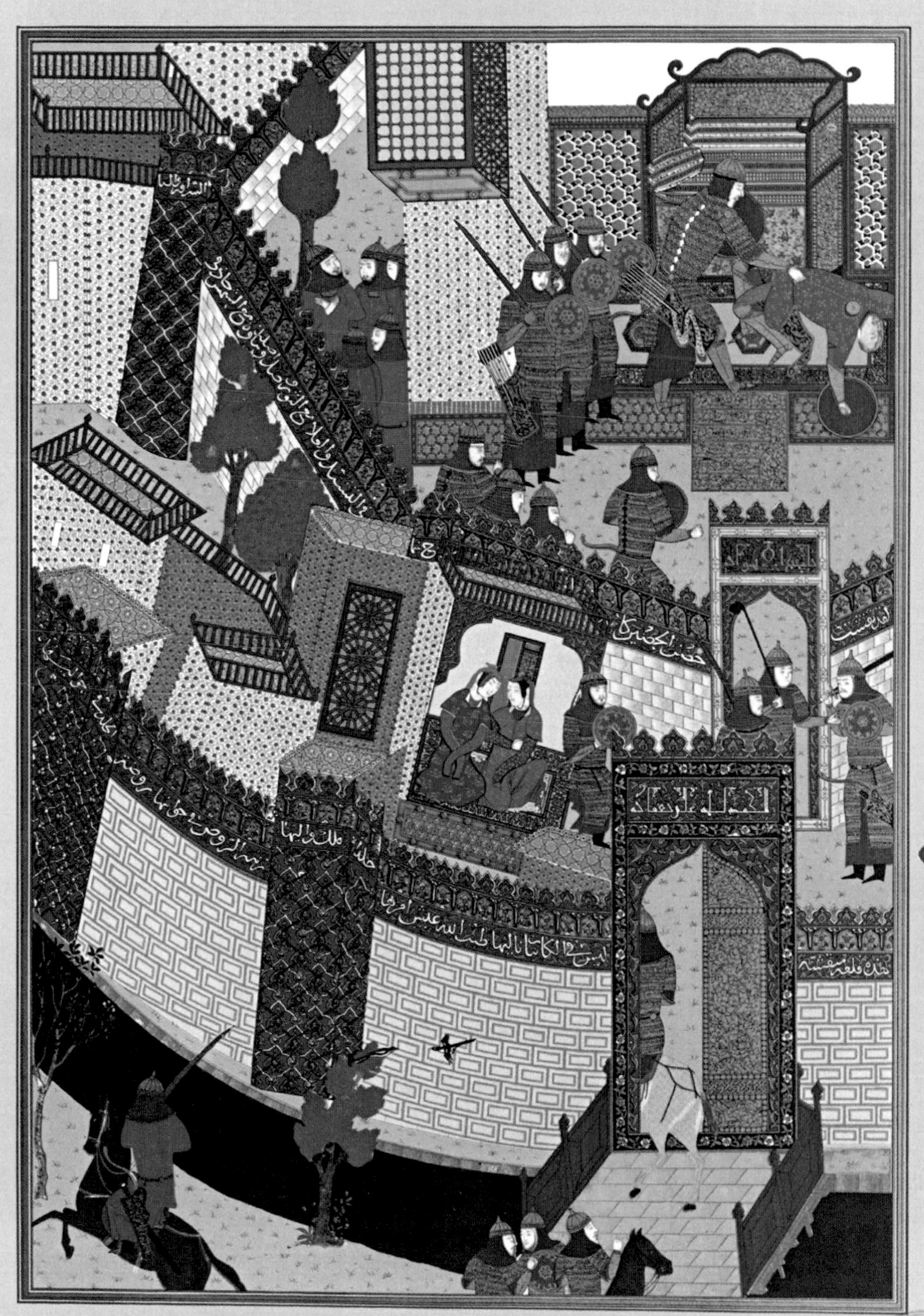

The seduction of Yusuf

Afghanistan (Herat), opaque watercolors, ink, gold on paper, entire page 30.5 x 21.5 cm
Cairo, National Library and Archives of Egypt

This miniature comes from a manuscript written by Sultan Ali al-Katib for the Timurid Prince Husain Baiqara Mirza (1470–1506) and illustrated by Bihzad (1450/1460–1535), the most famous painter in the Herat school. The picture shows a scene from the 1257 verse epic *Bustan* ("Garden of Taste") by Saadi (c. 1190–1283 or 1291). This tells the story of Zulaikha's attempt to seduce Yusuf as she takes him into each of her palace's seven rooms, always locking the door behind him, until they finally reach the inner apartment at the center. Here she wants to embrace him. However Yusuf flees without having touched the Princess. The painter indicates Yusuf's importance by way of a halo of flames, but the man and the woman are basically an unimportant detail. The real main motif is the splendid architecture in which the artist has embedded the action. Zulaikha's palace is mentioned in *Bustan* but there is a fuller description in *Haft Aurang* ("The Seven Thrones") by Jami (1414–1492) written just before the miniature was produced. For Jami the palace and its seven rooms symbolize the splendor of the material world, but that is also linked with mystical ideas. The seven rooms stand for a spiritual journey towards understanding. Bihzad's depiction probably derived inspiration from that interpretation of the story.

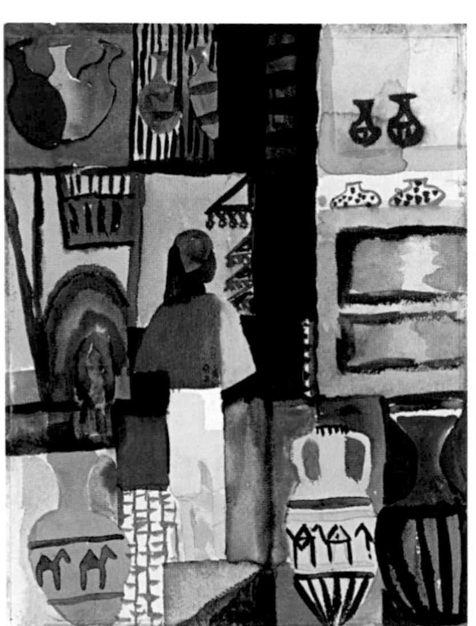

August Macke, Merchant with Jugs, Tunis, 1914

The painter presents part of the complex palace building where interior and exterior views are combined. Full of nooks and crannies, and surrounded by walls, this edifice extends over several levels, revealing rooms and halls with open or closed doors and linked by staircases. Such details as the brick walls and the faience mosaic may accord with the architecture of the time, but are in reality inventions by an artist uninterested in realism.

The watercolor by August Macke (1887–1914), presented in comparison with the Timurid miniature, exemplifies the dominance of flat surfaces in the work of Rhineland Expressionists. One source of that tendency was certainly the theories of French Cubists and Fauves to which Macke devoted intense study. However the structuring of volume and space in oriental art provided another model. A contiguity of various perspectives and viewpoints, and sometimes also an absolute convergence of spatiality and two-dimensionality, was to be encountered time and again – particularly in Persian miniatures which Macke saw in the 1910 Munich exhibition *Masterpieces of Muhammadan Art*. French modernism and Oriental depiction of space came together and led him to development of his own ideas.

"Yesterday we were in the various Arab red light districts. The women sat or stood in sunlit doorways. That looked splendid – as colorful and clear as a church window."

August Macke, letter dated 10 April 1914, to Elisabeth Macke

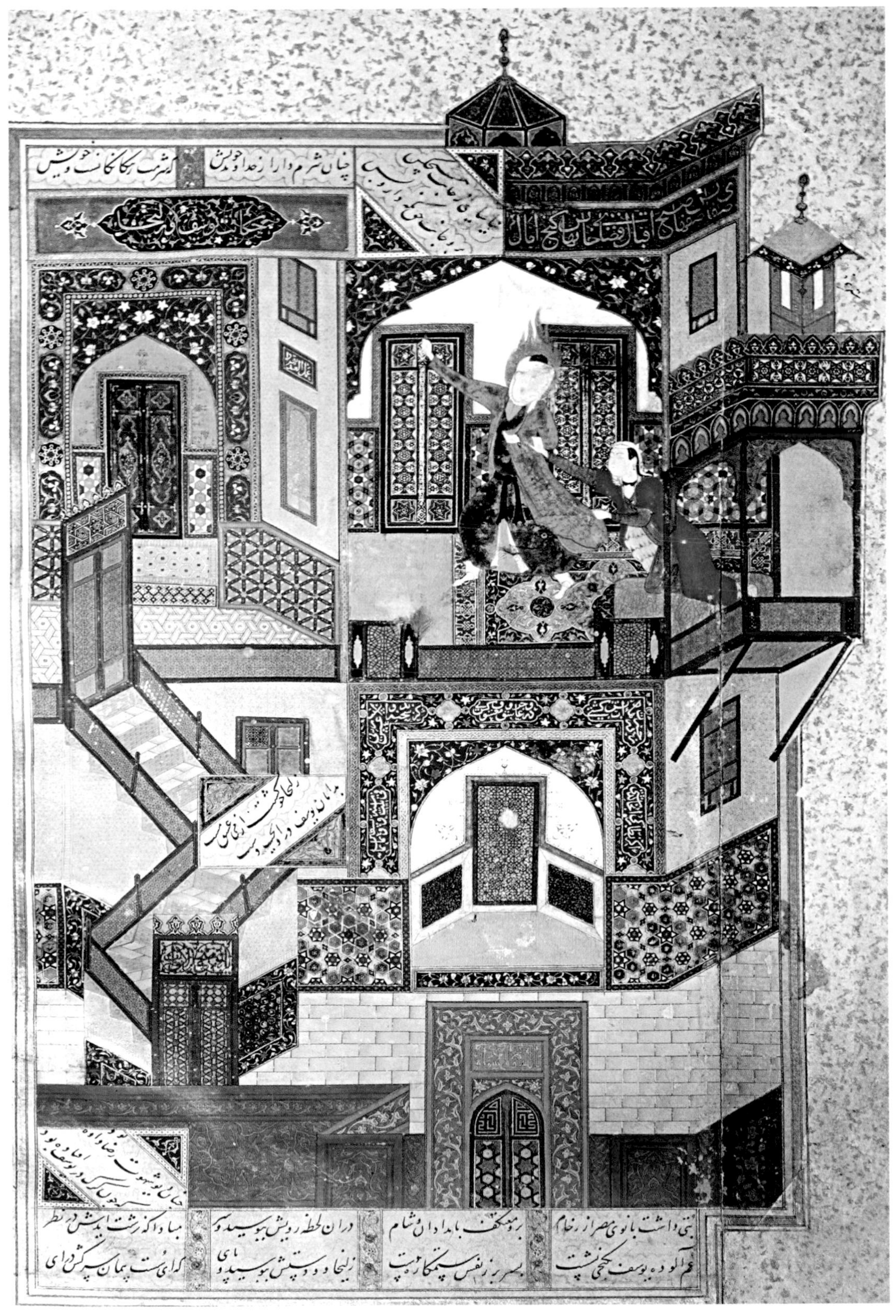

Harun al-Rashid in a Bath-House

Afghanistan (Herat), opaque watercolors, ink, gold on paper, entire page 25 x 17 cm (detail)
London, The British Library

The story illustrated here, the 19th in the *Makhzan al-Asrar* ("Treasury of Mysteries") from the *Khamsa* ("Five Stories") by Nizami (1141–1209), tells of an encounter between Caliph Harun al-Rashid (786–809) and a barber who asks to marry the ruler's daughter. Here the poet is speaking metaphorically about purity of soul, which is compared with a treasure allowing humans to express the boldest of thoughts.

This miniature, structured in an unusual gradated format, offers a look at the two main rooms in a Persian bath. The painter attempts to communicate perspective and spatial depth, for instance by the shadows in the left-foreground niche or the diagonal placing of the side-wall in the right-hand room. All the walls are adorned with tiles creating geometrical patterns and plant-like ornamentation. The left side is lit by two oil-lamps. The significance of the multicolored spherical shapes on the left-hand wall in the central room remains uncertain. This might involve colorful ornamentation or light streaming in through colored window-panes.

The furnishing of the two rooms is precisely observed – and so too are the actions of the people in the bath-house and the necessary utensils. Above the entrance a watchman looks down on what is happening in the main room where a number of men are undressing. Beneath him an attendant is using a long stick to hang up towels to dry. That directs the observer's gaze upwards and then onwards into the second room where the Caliph, the only seated figure, is to be seen, having his head shaved by a barber. Alongside, an assistant has water ready in a small brass bowl. The two beardless men in the foreground also make use of similar bowls for cleansing themselves. A calm atmosphere prevails despite the many people present in the scenery – since the arrangement of figures is well thought-through and balanced. Nevertheless, the men's diversity of movement generates liveliness.

The manuscript from which this miniature comes was made in Herat for Emir Ali Farsi Barlas, an officer at the court of Sultan Husain Baiqara (1470–1506). At the beginning of the 17th century it reached India in the library of Moghul Emperor Jahangir (1605–1627), who assumed that some of the miniatures could have been by Bihzad (1450/1460–1535), Persia's most celebrated painter.

Many of the 22 illustrations in the manuscript conceal the names of well-known Persian artists. That was not done by the painters themselves, but dates from a later period. Up to now, these miniatures can only be provisionally attributed to individual artists since a personal style in Islamic painting first developed about 100 years later. Someone like Bihzad worked closely with other artists and, as head of the workshop of Safavid rulers Shah Ismail (1501–1524) and Shah Tahmasp (1524–1576), greatly influenced the work of other masters so that it is often difficult to distinguish between them. Nevertheless, in this miniature the unusual choice of theme, perspectival depiction of the architecture, and the well-devised composition could well point towards Bihzad.

"At night when in her black hair, fragrant with roses, the heavens appeared as a bride with the Pleiades adorning her delicate ear ..."

Jami, Yusuf and Zulaikha, 1483

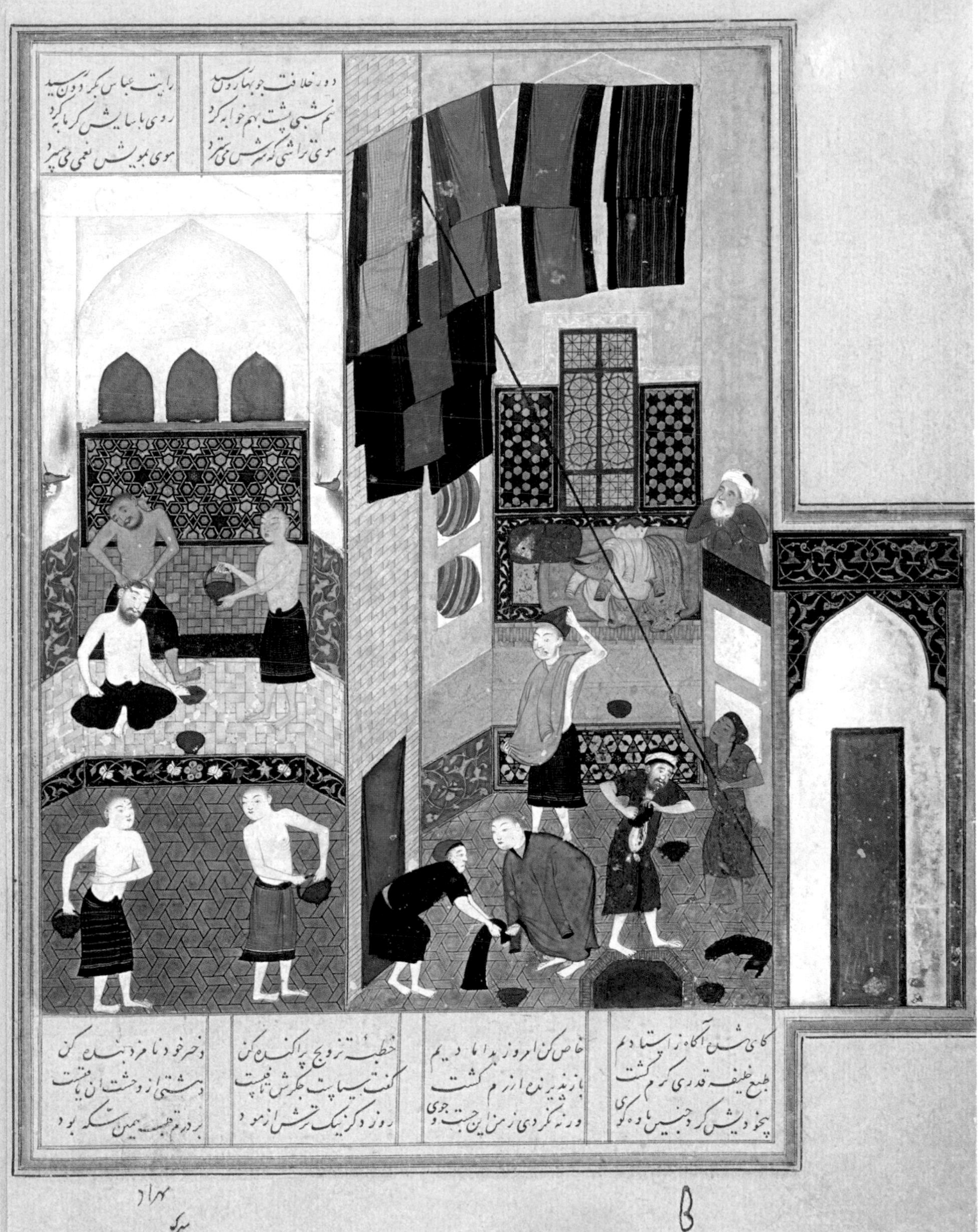

Nurshivan Listens to owls in a Ruined Palace

Iran (Tabriz), opaque watercolors, ink, gold on paper, miniature 30.4 x 19.4 cm
London, The British Library

The manuscript of Nizami's *Khamsa* ("Five Stories") containing this miniature was produced during the Safavid period for Shah Tahmasp I (1524–1576). The picture is signed "Mi... Musavvir" and dated on the building's white wall. That probably refers to Mir Musavvir (d. 1555) but the style indicates that the concept and important parts of the implementation were by Aqa Mirak (d. before 1576; see p. 75).

The episode on which the painting is based, comes from the *Makhzan al-Asrar* ("Treasury of Mysteries") section of the *Khamsa* (see ill. p. 71) concerned with the significance of this life and the life to come. The scene shows the Persian-Sassanid King Khusrau I Anushirwan (531–579) who gets separated from his retinue during a hunt and, accompanied only by his Vizier, comes across an abandoned city in ruins. The Prince (in a red robe) is recognizable from his precious weapons and richly accoutered horse. The Vizier, wearing a blue cloak, is riding on a mule. In answer to his question about what the two owls (to the left on a dilapidated roof) are talking about, the King overhears a prophesy. One of the owls promises, her daughter will marry the other's son, but demands a dowry. The second owl declares her willingness to give this ruined city and others, too, as a dowry if the ruler continues to neglect his country. The owls thus prophesied that Persia would soon be in ruins, just like the palace they inhabit, if the King does not renounce his passion for hunting and pleasure, and return to a path of virtue. With this moralizing declaration the text takes up traditional Persian ideals where a King's most important duty is to provide for his country's well-being.

The main emphasis in this picture is on the transience of all human culture. Rarely in Persian painting has an atmosphere of decline and abandonment been more movingly expressed by way of ruins. The tiles of a once wealthy palace are falling from the walls and lie scattered in the grass and in the building that nature has already regained. The impression of decline is even further intensified by the two men in the foreground, chopping down and sawing up olive trees. When the olive tree, symbolizing agricultural wealth, is destroyed, culture is reduced to rack and ruin. The birds serve to reinforce the image of abandonment. In Persian poetry owls symbolize despair and the storks nesting on the ruin indicate that in this palace no one will disturb these birds any longer.

This picture thus succeeds in giving expression to the text's symbolic and philosophical ideas. The painter also simultaneously created an idyllic landscape, the solitude of which is full of attractive motifs.

"If our worthy sovereign persists in his present courses, and leaves his people to perish in misery and neglect, I will gladly give not two or three but a hundred thousand ruined villages."

Nizami, 1174

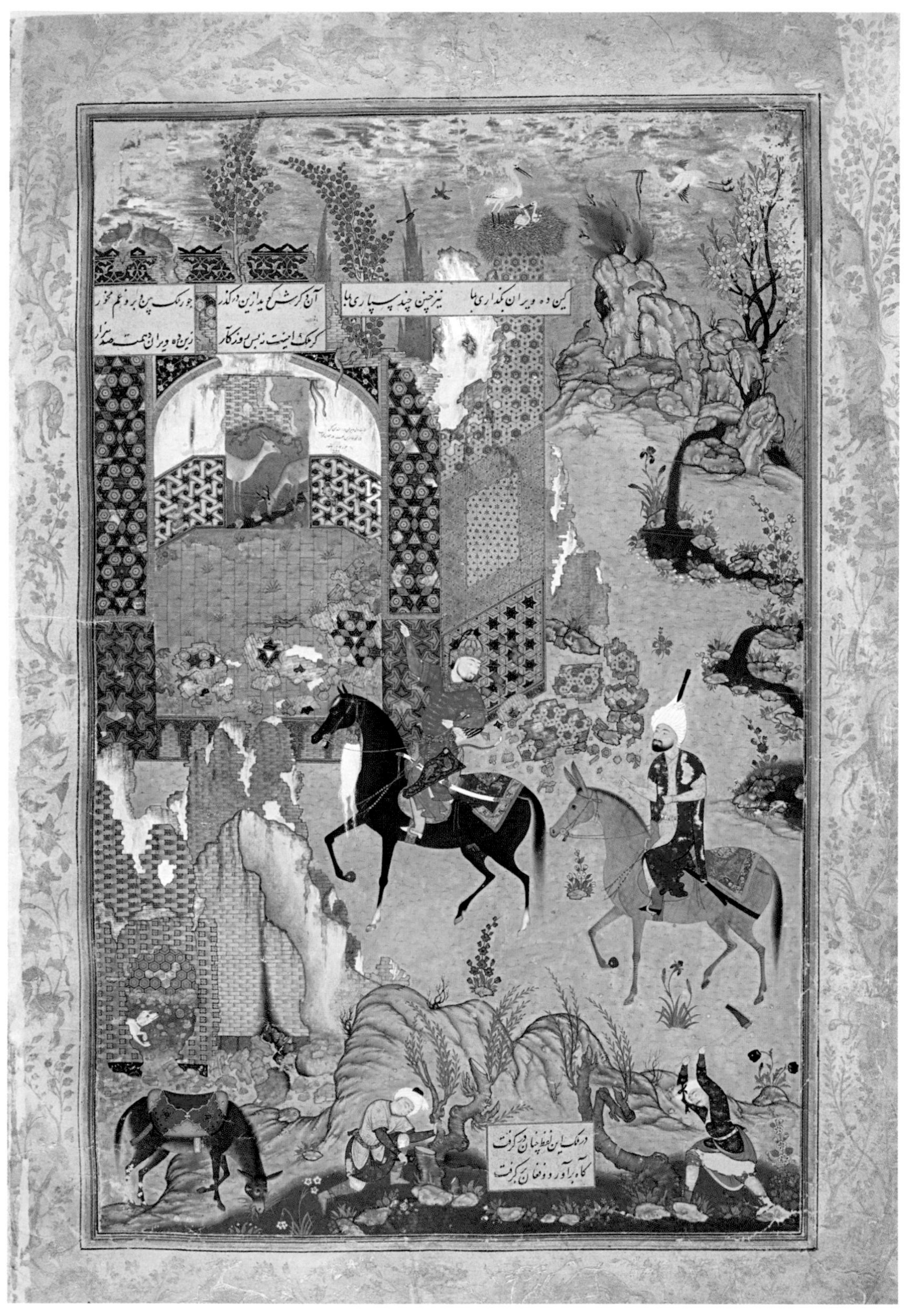

A King Driven out of a saint's Tomb

Iran (Tabriz or Qazwin), opaque watercolors, ink, gold on paper, 59.7 x 45.1 cm
Geneva, Aga Khan Trust for Culture

Aqa Mirak (d. before 1576), who is thought to have painted this picture, was a personal friend of Safavid ruler Shah Tahmasp (1524–1576) and one of the leading artists at his court. Many of his works have survived (see ill. p. 73), including some with his own signature. The miniature presented here is part of a manuscript of Nizami's (1141–1209) *Khamsa*, which was probably the last manuscript commissioned by Shah Tahmasp before (in 1556) religious convictions led to his turning away from visual art.

This scene illustrates a story from the *Falnama* ("Book of Prophecies"), a compilation of stories, verse, and predictions. All these texts are of a moralizing nature. They tell of pre-Islamic demons and Kings, but also of Adam and Eve and of the Prophet Muhammad's journey to heaven. The text accompanying this depiction is intended to warn Kings that they should respect and uphold the law.

A domed building with two minarets and a walled courtyard, also containing the grave, is to be seen in a hilly landscape. The patterning on the outer walls makes clear that this is obviously intended as depiction of a historic edifice. It is made of brick with geometrical ornamentation, i.e. employs a technique no longer used in the 16th century. Even though this building includes some three-dimensional elements, it is not a realistic representation of architecture as the main scene shows. This plays in a completely two-dimensional stage-like area, adorned with metal lamps and textile hangings with religious inscriptions. In the foreground a group of people is standing around a sarcophagus covered with cloths, which is the actual grave of the saint revered here. A side wall has opened up and a hand flings out flames to expel from this shrine a crowned and armed King. This King rushes towards the way out, swinging his sword and casting a last furious look towards the grave. The four gesticulating men behind the sarcophagus and other persons – observing from windows, doorways, and the rooftop – are indignant about what is happening. Even a group of men visible on the hill behind the sanctuary are shocked and upset.

This miniature is notable for the vitality and feeling for drama with which the entire situation is presented. The gestures and expressions of those present reveal their feelings in many ways, and the figure of the fleeing King with its ponderous and explicit movements is deliberately contrasted with the other personages' more elegant bodies. Such a way of representation reflects the artist's talent for depicting individual figures, which made Aqa Mirak one of the most famous painters and portraitists of his time.

Persian miniatures were admired by European representatives of Classical Modernism in the early 20th century and utilized as sources of principles. After he had seen such works in the 1910 *Masterpieces of Muhammadan Art* exhibition at Munich, Wassily Kandinsky wrote: "It was as if a curtain had parted before one, revealing a new depth of happiness."

"Build up the desert of those deprived of bliss; there is no better building in this ruined world than this."

Mir Musavvir, 1539/1540

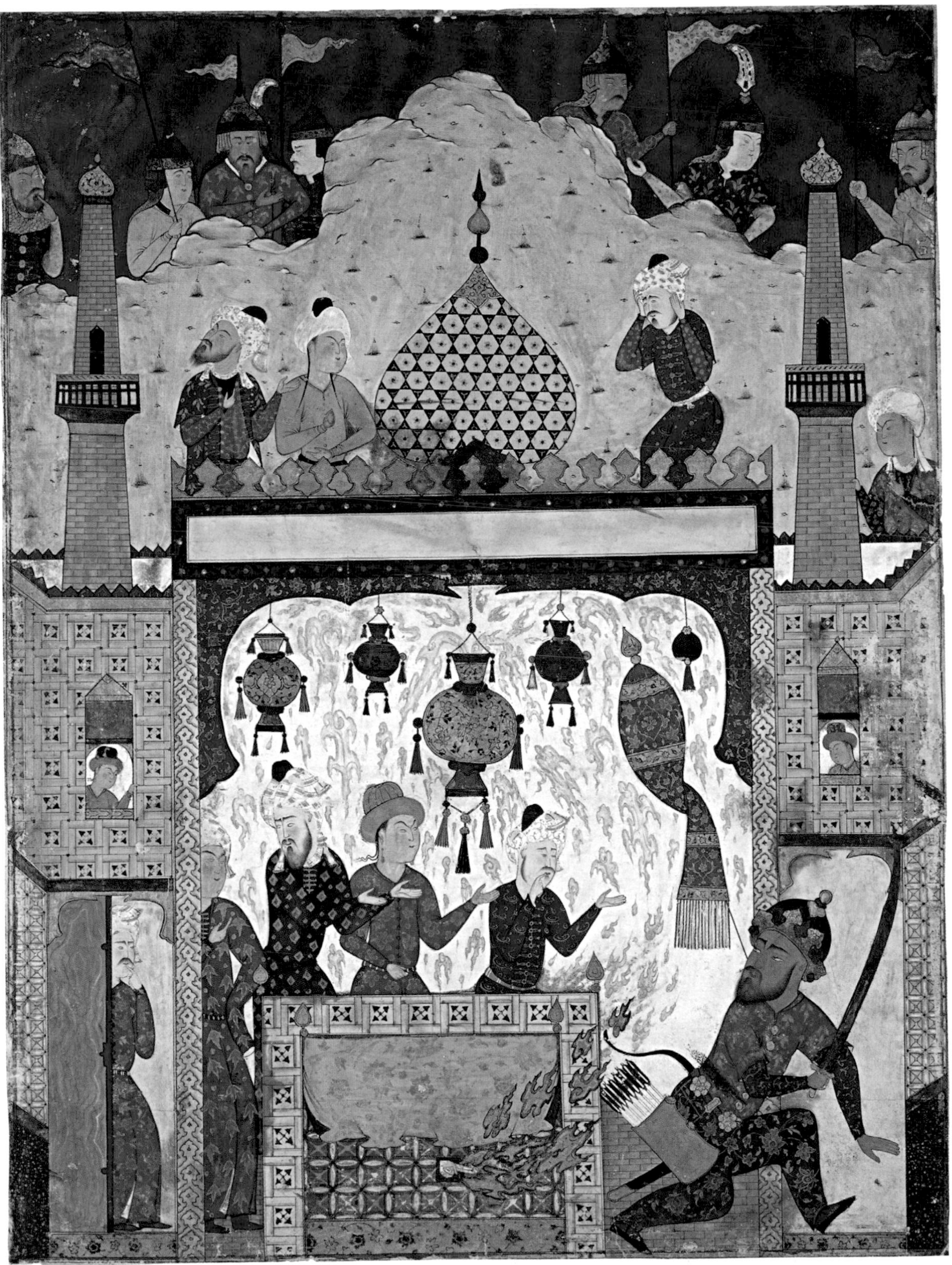

The Ardabil carpet

Iran (Tabriz?), knotted carpet, silk and wool, 10.51 x 5.34 m
London, Victoria and Albert Museum

One of the largest and most important of classical Persian carpets is known as the "Ardabil carpet". It was designed by Maqsud Kashani. This carpet is said to come from Ardabil in Northern Persia, a Shiite place of pilgrimage where the mausoleum and mosque-tomb of Sheikh Safi al-Din (1251–1334), ancestor of the Safavid Dynasty, form part of a group of buildings.

With its huge dimensions and the astonishing delicacy of the knotting, the carpet is a masterpiece of this Persian art. Its ornamentation is structured within a central field and a framing border. The inner field is filled by a multilayered system of arabesques with blossoms on a dark-blue ground. At the centre is a yellow medallion with 16 points – to which differently colored little oval medallions are attached. Identical quarter medallions, also crammed with tiny oval likenesses, fill the four corners. The two large mosque lamps depicted on the longitudinal axis, each hanging on four chains from one of the oval medallions, are unique in the ornamentation of oriental carpets. The outer delimitation of the main field consists of a multistriated border, in the middle of which cartouches and overlapping tracery alternate.

This pattern is extremely precise in all its details and that, together with the balance of colors, indicates that this carpet was made in a court workshop, following a carefully drawn design. More detailed information is provided by a white cartouche on the edge of one of the inner field's smaller sides where a couplet by Hafiz (d. 1390), the Persian poet, is quoted: "I have no other place of refuge in this world apart from Your threshold. My head has no other resting-place except for this gateway". That verse is followed by the words: "Made by Maqsud Kashani, servant of the threshold, in the year 946". Maqsud Kashani obviously devised a cartoon as basis for the knotting of this carpet in Northern Persia. It might have been commissioned by Shah Tahmasp I (1524–1576), the Safavid ruler.

It is thanks to the English designer William Morris (1834–1896) that this carpet is in London today. From the 1870s Morris was the Victoria and Albert Museum's expert for oriental carpets. His personal commitment established the financial basis for the Museum's purchase of this carpet in 1893. Morris was very enthusiastic about this work and described its design as being "of unique perfection and beauty".

Morris also took oriental ornamentation into account in his own designs for carpets. However, he changed the structure of the arabesques and in the borders of his carpets combined oriental blossoms with forms from Italian Renaissance art. Even though the oriental models were simplified, Morris took over the underlying formal principles of division of spatial areas – such as utilization of a framing element bordering the inner pattern.

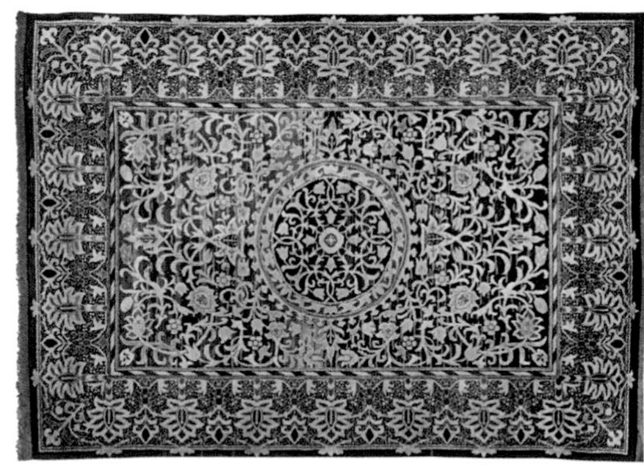
William Morris, the "Hammersmith" Carpet, 1887

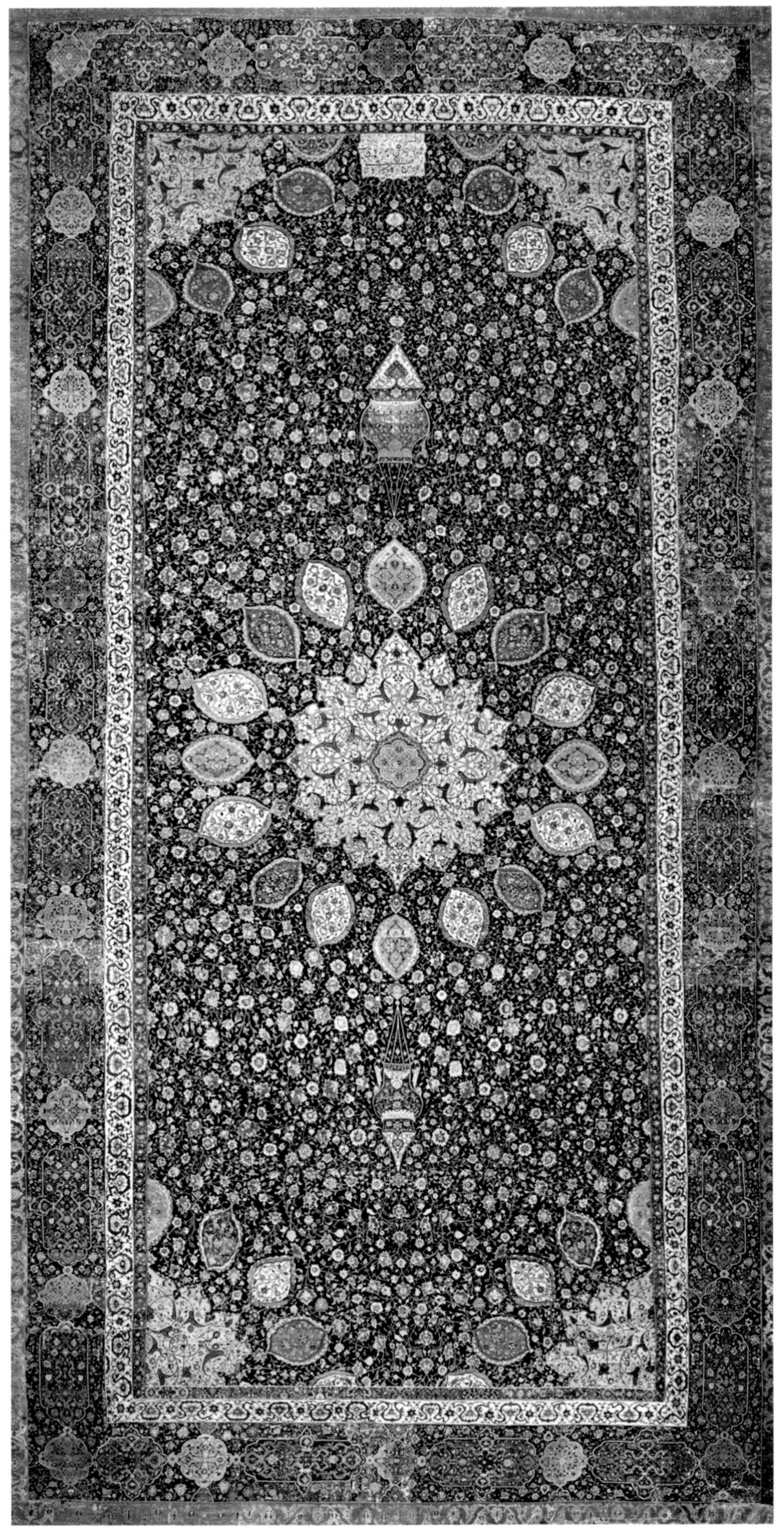

MIR AFZAL TUNI (AFZAL AL-HUSAYNI) c. 1640/1645

A Lady watches her Dog Drinking

Iran (Isfahan), watercolor, opaque watercolors, and gold on paper, miniature 11.9 x 15.8 cm (detail)
London, The British Museum

During the first half of the 17th century the Safavid court at Isfahan was extremely open to the world and that also found expression in its art. At that time more and more Europeans came to Iran, including a number of artists who influenced Persian painters. In addition, the works of the great Safavid painter Riza (Aqa Riza or Riza'iya 'Abbasi, d. 1635) exerted a lasting impact on succeeding generations.

One of Riza's most gifted successors was the artist who signed this miniature with the name Afzal Tuni, who was also known as Afzal al-Husayni. He was active at the court of Shah Abbas II (1642–1666), where he created decorative individual pages for collective albums and was commissioned by the ruler to work on illustrations for a splendid *Shahnama* manuscript. The page shown here presents a beautiful young woman against the background of a delicately golden landscape. She is lying on two cushions and observing how her little dog drinks out of a bowl. At the woman's feet is a Chinese-style vase with a bouquet of roses, and on the ground in front of her are a shallow bowl and a smaller container. The young woman's robe is pushed up, revealing her strikingly patterned trousers and her stomach. The golden background and her expensive clothing suggest great luxury, and her pose, the greedy way the little dog is drinking, and the loving way its owner looks at the animal betray eroticism and desire.

In this depiction the painter closely followed two pictures by Riza. The motif of the little dog drinking was taken over from the last miniature Riza painted, in 1634. That shows a young man in European clothing who gets his little white dog to drink wine out of a bowl. Mir Afzal Tuni replaced the young European by a woman whose pose he found in another picture by Riza. This was probably done around 1595 and showed a sleeping woman in a transparent robe lying exactly as in the later representation. There Riza followed a European model. This pose was originally based on an engraving from Rome by Marcantonio Raimondi around 1520–1525, following an original by Raphael (1483–1520).

In both its motifs and style this miniature is very close to Riza's work, but there are also clear references to European influences in the shading and modeling of the woman's face and the sturdy physicality of her limbs. In addition, the roses in the vase behind her are reminiscent of Western depictions.

This work thus exemplifies a representation which must have seemed both luxurious and highly exotic in 17th century Persian art with its unusual (European) pose, a Chinese vase, and two direct citations from Riza brought together in a unified composition.

"The beauty of a thing lies in the appearance of that perfection which is realizable and in accord with its nature. When all possible traits of perfection appear in an object, it presents the highest degree of beauty ..."

Al-Ghazali, Kimiya al Sa'ada ("The Elixir of Bliss")

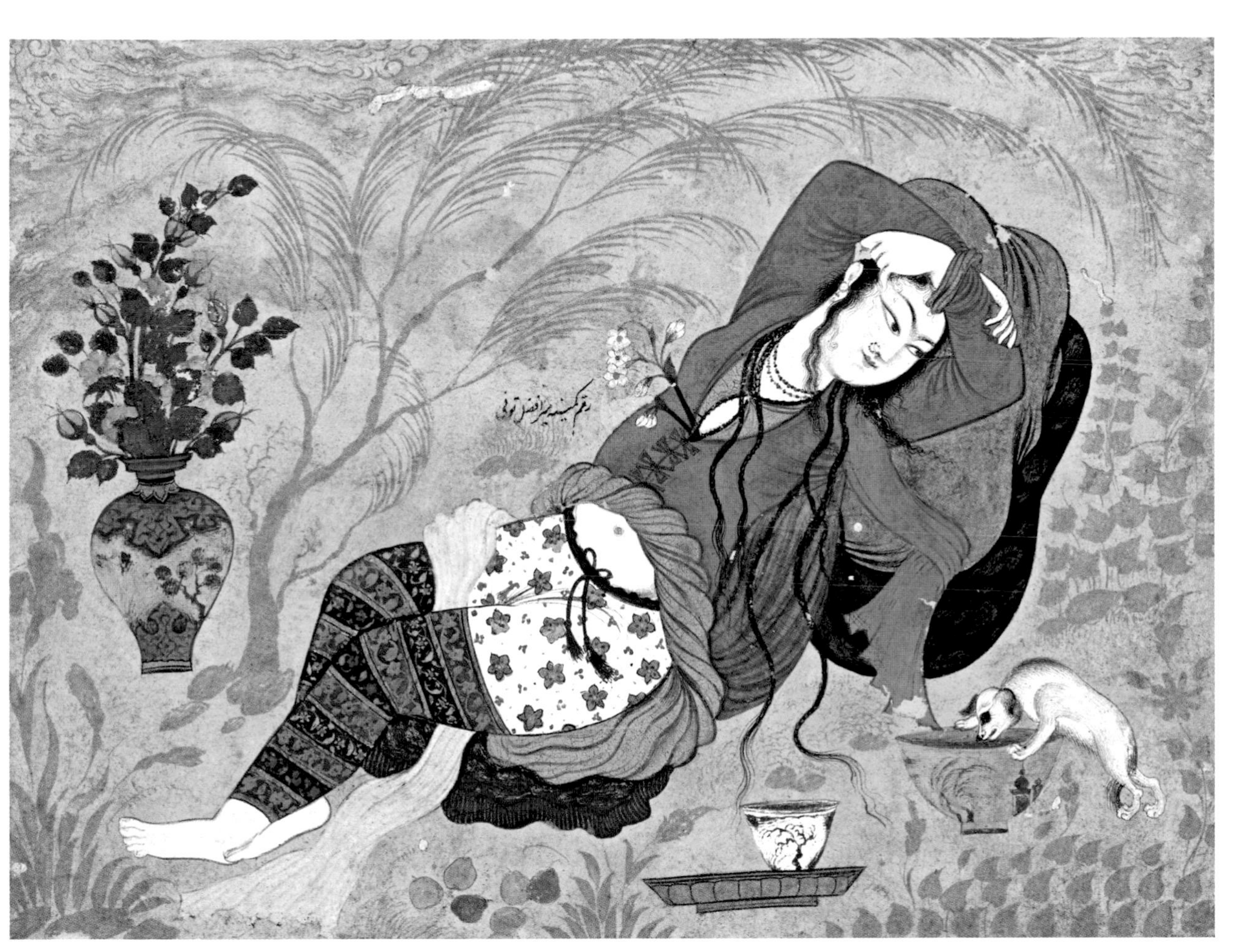
رقم کمینه میر افضل تونی

calligraphic ornamentation

With the Words "No Hero except Ali and No Sword apart from Dhu l-faqar"
Iran, *Thuluth* script, ink, gold on paper, 16 x 24.5 cm; from a collective album
Berlin, Staatliche Museen zu Berlin – Stiftung Preussischer Kulturbesitz, Museum of Islamic Art

Several stages of work were required in creating this calligraphy produced during the Safavid period (1501–1732). First the broad black outlines of the letters were delineated on the white paper, these were then filled with Indian ink, using a brush. This technique is different from the method employed in other Iranian calligraphy which was usually written with a reed pen. In the final stage the outlines of letters were highlighted with gold and accentuated. This highly artistically arranged text begins in the middle of the page and must then be read in different directions: horizontally, vertically, and diagonally. The elegant *Thuluth* ("a third") script, here used in an unconventional way, is strikingly malleable and the slender proportions of individual letters are distributed on the page in a balanced and harmonious way. The name of this script derives from the official style, where other letters were not permitted to be more than a third of its height.

This Iranian calligraphy reached India because of its unusual composition. There it was mounted on a larger backing in the 18th century and bound into a collective album – at the request of a European collector – where miniatures alternated with calligraphic ornamentation.

The text of this calligraphy runs: *La fatan illa 'aliyun, la saifun illa dhu l-faqar* ("No Hero except Ali and No Sword apart from Dhu l-faqar"). That is the most frequent inscription on Islamic swords and sabers and a Shia victory cry, especially for Dervishes and members of religious orders. Ali (d. 661) was Muhammad's son-in-law who, after the first Muslims fled from Mecca to Medina, became one of the Prophet's most important comrades-in-arms in the struggle against the Arab Quraysh tribe in the Battle of Badr (624). He is revered as a victorious champion of religious truth as well as exemplifying great piety and learning. His speeches and conversations, collected in *Nahj al-Balagha* ("The Way of Eloquence"), provided the basis for classical Arab grammar and long served as a model for correct utilization of Arabic. The division of Muslims into Sunnis and Shiites started during Ali's Caliphate. The latter believe that the succession to the Prophet can only be assumed by members of his family and therefore see Ali as the first legitimate Caliph.

According to Islamic tradition, *Dhu l-faqar*, the sword mentioned in this calligraphy, was seized by Muhammad during the Battle of Badr. This double-edged weapon later came into the possession of Ali and became one of the oldest and best-known symbols of Islam.

"[Remember how] thy Lord brought thee forth from thy house with the truth, and a part of the believers were averse to it, disputing with thee concerning the truth after it had become clear, as though they were being driven into death with their eyes wide open."

Qur'an, Sura 8, verses 5/6, on the Battle of Badr

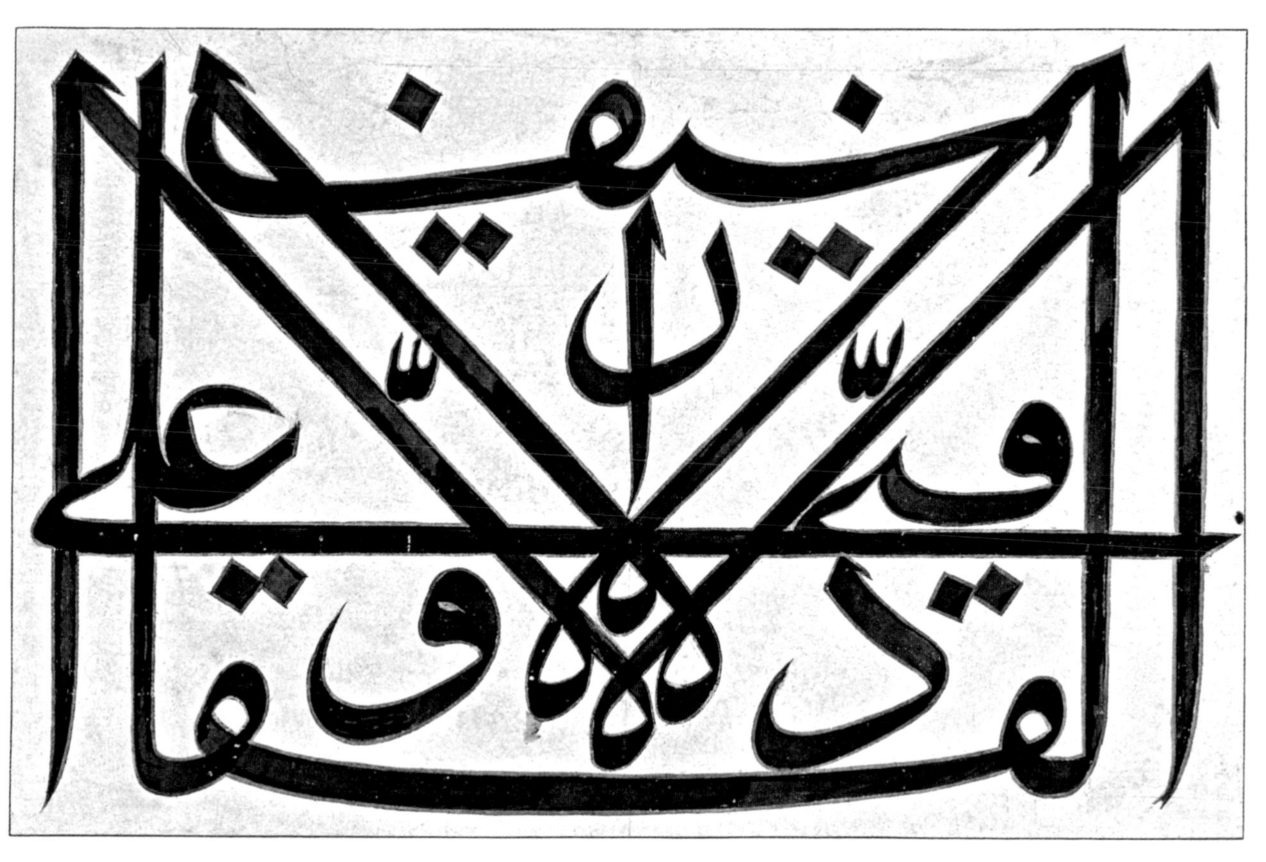

UNKNOWN TURKISH CERAMICIST

c. 1480

Plate

Turkey (Iznik), quartz ceramic painted beneath the glaze, diameter 44.5 cm
Den Haag, Gemeentemuseum

This large cobalt-blue plate is completely covered with stylized ornamentation and floral motifs. At its centre is a little rosette set within entwined blossoms on slender spiraling stems. Superimposed on this pattern is a complex overlapping of lancet leaves. Similar tendrils, framing eight symmetrically placed pinnate motifs, are to be found in the intermediate section of the plate. At regular intervals between these two different kinds of leaves are stylized palmette blossoms with more flowering tendrils, intersected above and below by the lancet leaves. The narrow outer edge of the plate is adorned with wave-like tendrils and blossoms large and small, and outside are peonies following the Chinese model.

The plate is made of quartz chip – i.e. white clay and quartz to which liquid lead-alkali is added as usual in Iznik. The form made from this material is thinly coated with white as the base for painting, and then the decorated plate is glazed.

In its color the ornamented plate is reminiscent of the Chinese porcelain that was imported into the Islamic world from the second half of the 14th century and highly esteemed there. The blue-and-white ware of the Yuan (1279–1368) and Early Ming (1368–1643) periods were particularly popular so that this style was maintained in China for the manufacture of export goods until the 16th century, even though thought old-fashioned in its country of origin. Large amounts of porcelain were mainly imported for use at the Istanbul court, and that is why today there are over 2,600 pieces from the Ming period in the Topkapi Palace collections.

It was the wish to imitate Chinese ware which led to further development of local ceramics in the Ottoman Empire. That mainly happened at Iznik but also elsewhere with production reaching a peak between 1480 and 1600. Even though Turkish artists found their own ways of ornamenting ceramics, they also continued to produce wares in blue and white, imitating the Chinese model. From the end of the 15th century there were complex patterns (like the one here) deploying arabesques, pinnate-lobed leaves, and lotus blossoms in those colors.

A fresh approach came in the 1530s. A group of Ottoman ceramicists developed multicolored decoration utilizing flower-motifs that were very natural in appearance. Roses, carnations, tulips, and hyacinths were mainly used for such ornamentation, and this became known as *Quatre Fleurs* style ("Four Flowers"). The term "Musli style" is also widespread today since a ceramicist working in that way used to sign his products with the name "Musli".

Both forms of ornamentation, the stylized blue-and-white and the brightly colorful "Musli", existed alongside one another during the 16th century, giving rise to masterpieces of Ottoman ceramics.

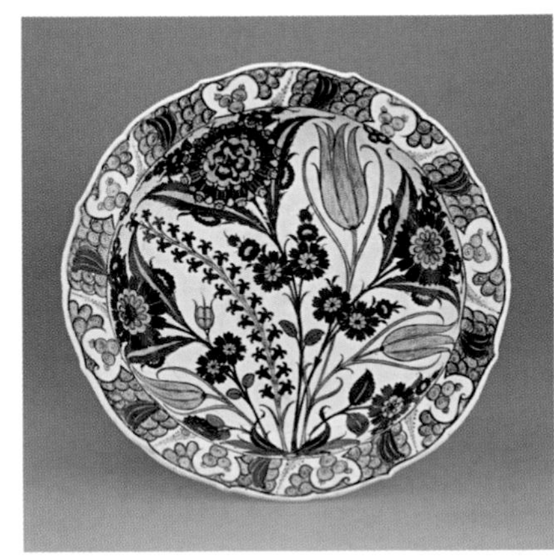

Plate, Turkey (Iznik), c. 1550

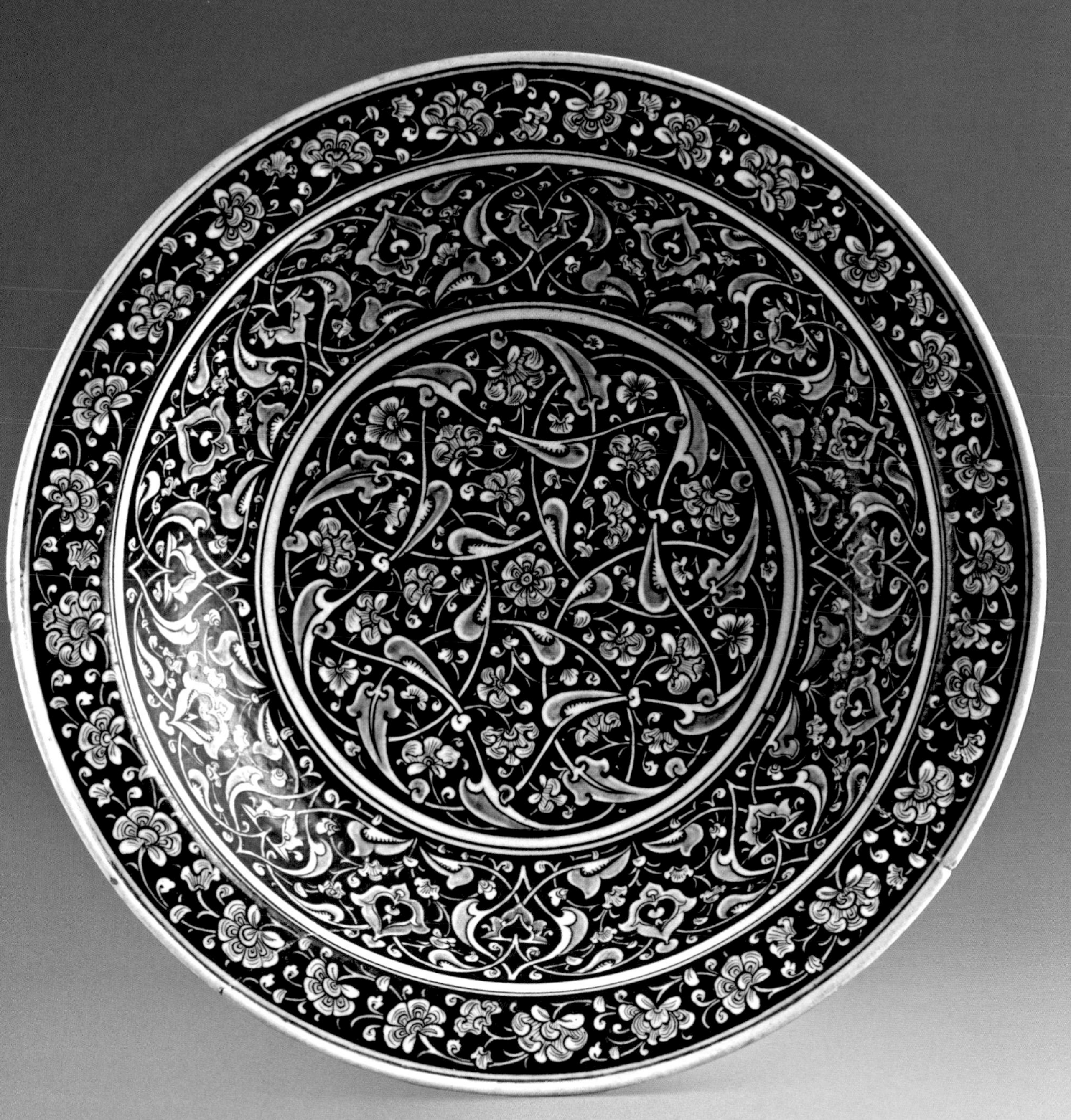

Kaftan

Turkey (Istanbul), silk, multicolored dyed satin, gilded metal threads, length 147 cm, arm length 117 cm
Istanbul, Topkapi Palace Museum

This kaftan is certainly one of the most precious textiles in the Islamic world. It was created for the Istanbul court, possibly for *Sehzade* ("Prince") Bayazid (d. 1561), the son of Sultan Suleyman II (1520–1566). Such special garments were worn during the most important official occasions at the Ottoman court, as recorded on 16th century miniatures.

This long-sleeved over-garment has a narrow collar around the neck opening. The material is cut straight as far as the waist and from there flared down to the hem. When putting on the kaftan, the two front parts wrap on top of one another without any fastening. Openings for the wearer's arms are at shoulder-height – but covered by the full false sleeves, reaching down to the ankles, which are put over the back when wearing the garment.

The silk from which the kaftan was made is embellished with a complicated pattern in *Saz* (pinna) style: multicolored ornamentation, consisting of lotus and peony blossoms, rosettes, plum blossom, and elegant feathery leaves, is set against a dark-brown, almost black ground. None of the flowers are depicted realistically. These are creations of pure imagination which take on radiant colorfulness against the dark background. All these blossoms are inspired by Chinese models, yet their specific form and combination is characteristic of the art of the Ottoman Empire. Particularly impressive here is the elegance of the depiction and the interaction between contrasting colors. It is difficult to decide whether the individual motifs within the pattern are symbolic. In general, they are intended to give expression to wealth and well-being.

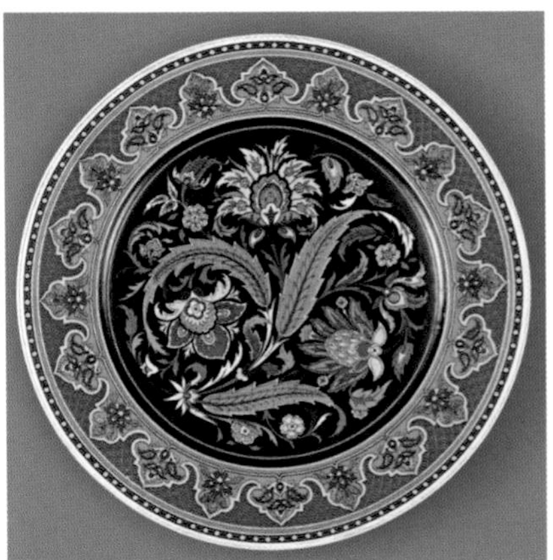

Villeroy & Boch, Stoneware Plate, decoration no. 1404, Germany (Mettlach), around 1885

The design certainly came from the court workshop in Istanbul, but it can be assumed that the material was woven at Bursa in West Turkey. The Ottoman center for the production of silk had long been established there and the technique of multicolored silk-weaving was also developed by Bursa workshops. Craftsmen took almost three years to make such a piece. Other examples of such a lavishly adorned garment are exceptionally rare. However, in later periods this kind of material was thought to be characteristic of the 16th century and therefore frequently shown on imaginary portraits of Ottoman Sultans. The flower patterns on this silk are closely related to contemporary tile ornamentation and book illustration.

From the second half of the 19th century many European producers of ceramics used the ornamentation on such pieces as models for their own products. Nevertheless, few firms really copied this kind of decoration. Among those which did venture on such complicated ornamentation was Villeroy & Boch (established at that time in Luxemburg and Mettlach) – as is shown in this plate, based on the Ottoman style from around 1550.

"Now come with me and direct your gaze towards the huge number of turbans with innumerable folds in the white silk – and towards the dazzling garments of every style and color, and everywhere there is the magnificence of gold, silver, purple, silk, and satin ... Never have I been presented with a more beautiful feast for the eyes."

Ogier Ghislain de Busbecq, Letters, 1558

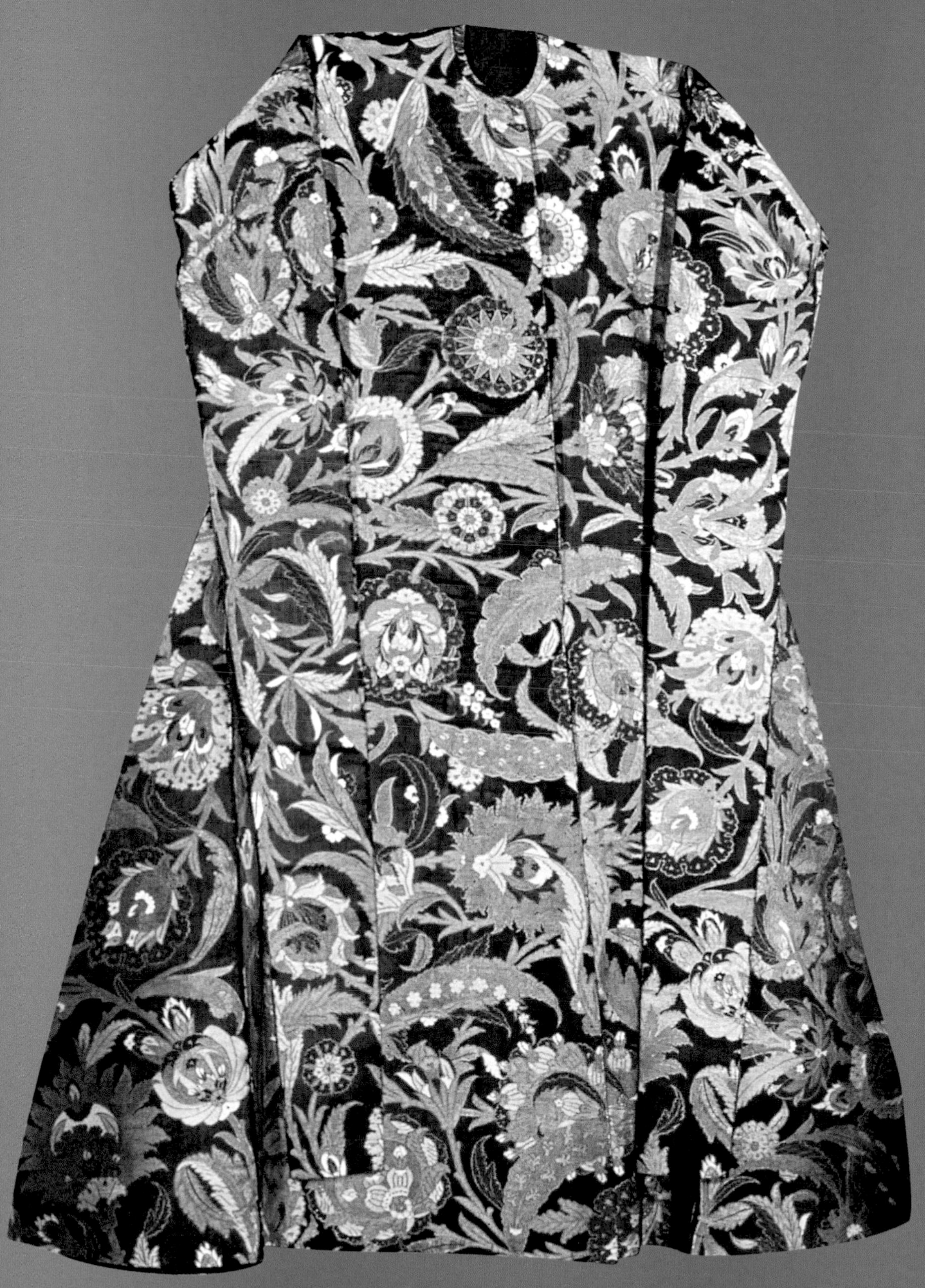

ANONYMOUS

2nd half of the 16th century

Prayer Mat

Turkey (Istanbul) or Egypt (Cairo), wool, cotton, silk, 181 x 127 cm
Vienna, MAK – Austrian Museum of Applied Arts / Contemporary Art

This prayer mat, which used to belong to the Austrian royal family, can be seen as the epitome of Ottoman style in the 16th century. It is not known who commissioned this work; nor is it clear to date whether the piece was made in Istanbul at the court workshops, or in Cairo, capital of the Ottoman province of Egypt.

The density of ornamentation demands that the observer take time in investigating the composition and its details. An inner area is clearly apparent, surrounded by a broad outer strip. The framing consists of two differently structured edgings of rosettes and a wide main border with ongoing entwining blossoms. In the upper part of the inner area is a symmetrical arch-like form standing for the niche pendentive. This motif is characteristic of Islamic prayer mats. However, comprehension of the architectural link is made more difficult by the bisection of the arch and the absence of the little pillars which frequently close the niche-form to the right and left. Instead, the lower border of this area contains quarter-medallions with tendrils of entwining clouds, which, in fact, come from the composition of medallion carpets. In other words, the pattern here was implemented completely independently of the architectural model and is to be seen as a textile composition with as many different motifs as possible.

The niche is decorated with light-blue arabesques on a white ground. The dark-red inner field is filled with a symmetrically structured plant composition. Blossoms extend along the middle axis, linked on both sides by way of tendrils and plant stems with curving spear-thistle leaves and diverse large blossoms, sometimes crossed by other vegetation. The broad border also presents blossoms and leaves on a light-blue ground. The repetition of light-blue and the carefully positioned tendrils around the four corners make apparent how thoughtfully devised the overall composition of the carpet was. The complex pattern was first drawn on a cartoon, which then served as basis for the knotting. The detailing of this design provides an exemplary demonstration of the *Saz* ("reed-stem") and *Quatre Fleurs* ("Four Flowers") motifs. Many works of art, including the famous tiles and ceramics from Iznik, court carpets, and silk garments, manifest this courtly style with its many leaves and blossoms.

If such a carpet were used as a prayer mat, the believer may have had the feeling of being in the garden of paradise. This piece was unused when it was acquired by the Hapsburgs – particularly appreciated as a precious masterpiece and kept in their possession. It was put on public display for the first time at the great Vienna carpet exhibition of 1891.

"Looking one day at an oriental carpet aglow with iridescent colors, and following with his eyes the silvery glints running across the weft of the wool, which was a combination of yellow and plum, he had thought what a good idea it would be to place on this carpet something that would move about and be dark enough to set off these gleaming tints."

Joris-Karl Huysmans, Against Nature, 1884

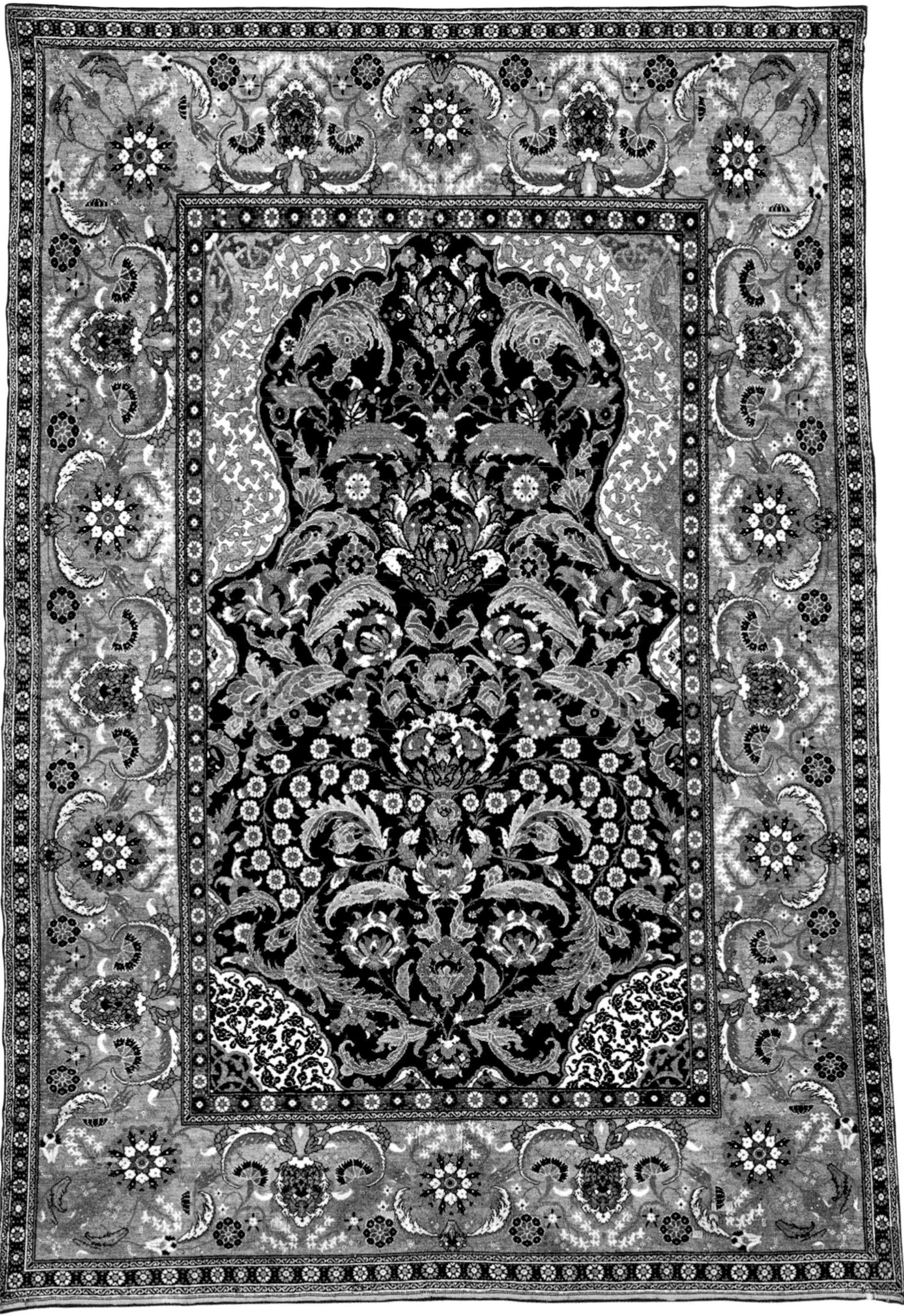

Misbah the Grocer Brings Parragan, a Spy, into his House

North India, miniature in pigment painting with gold on cotton, fixed on paper, entire page 70.8 x 54.9 cm
New York, NY, The Metropolitan Museum of Art

When he was just 14, the art-loving Mogul ruler Akbar I (1556–1605) commissioned illustration of the *Hamzanama*, a collection of stories about the magical deeds and adventures of Hamza ibn Ab al-Muttalib (b. 569), an uncle of the Prophet Muhammad. From 1558 onwards, around 100 Indian and Persian artists in the court workshop created 1,400 miniatures for this project, of which around 200 survive today. This venture was directed by two Persian painters, Mir Sayyid Ali (d.c. 1572) and Khwaja Abd al-Samad (active 1540–1595). In 1881 24 of these miniatures were discovered by Sir Caspar Purdon Clarke (1846–1911), director of the Victoria and Albert Museum in London, at a merchant's house in Srinagar, Kashmir, where they were used to draught-proof a window.

The image here illustrates an episode from the story about the abduction of Hamza's son Ibrahim by Firuz, a spy. Hamza sends Parragan, one of his own spies, into the city to find Ibrahim. Parragan disguises himself as a merchant and meets Misbah, a pious grocer, who takes him home and advises him on how the abducted boy could be freed. This giving of advice is depicted in the miniature. Misbah is depicted as being bigger and more voluminous than the other characters so as to indicate his singular importance for further development of the story.

Parragan is crouching in an *iwan* ("a hall open to the front"), alongside an inner courtyard, and talking to Misbah, who is sitting next to him. The floor of this hall is covered with an Indian carpet and on its walls are weapons, shields, flags, and animal skins. The arrows, swords, and daggers hanging down between Parragan and Misbah seem particularly threatening, underlining how dangerous this situation is.

Expensively dressed armed men are sitting and standing in the courtyard, listening to what the two main characters are saying. Servants bring food in ceramic dishes with brass lids, and in precious vessels. Water is served in a brass can with calligraphic ornamentation. Ceramic tiles are to be seen on the floor, arranged in a geometrical star-like pattern.

Paintings were usually a group project. In this case most of the work was by Mithra (16th century), but the two main figures were painted by Dasavanta (d. 1584), one of the best 16th century Indian artists whose talent was discovered and furthered by Akbar himself (see ill. p. 90). The reverse of each image contains the text for the following miniature. Their style makes these *Hamzanama* miniatures a key work in the art of the Mogul period since they link elements from the Indian tradition with aspects of Persian painting and also influences from European models. They thus mark the start of development of an autonomous Mogul art. The large format and lavish implementation of these works are also remarkable in conjunction with their stylistic quality. Cotton stuck to paper was used for a mount and then the miniatures were stored loose in chests (rather than being bound together) from which individual sheets were taken as required.

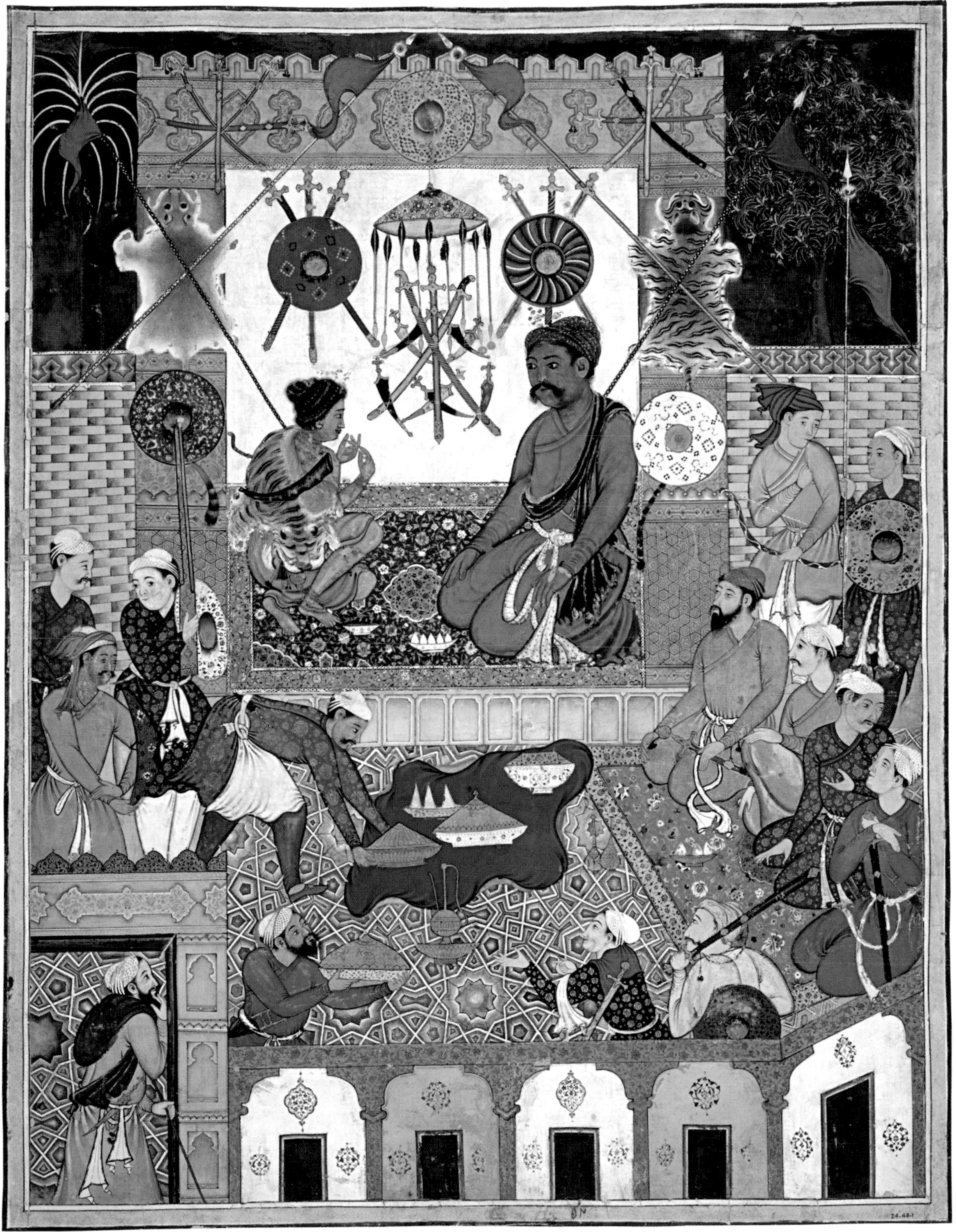

IKHLAS AND MADHU (MADHU KHANZAD) c. 1600

Akbar crossing the Ganges

North India, watercolors and gold on paper, entire page 33.4 x 19 cm
London, Victoria and Albert Museum

Among the most important manuscripts originating in the court of the Mogul Emperors was a copy of the *Akbarnama* ("History of Akbar") containing an account of the reign of Akbar I (1556–1605), commissioned by the ruler's closest adviser, Abu l-Fazl Allami (d. 1602) and produced around 1589. This manuscript also contains remarks about the artists who made the many illustrations. Akbar himself decided which scenes should be illustrated and had individual pictures produced as a cooperative venture involving several artists. Most of the miniatures shown here was the work of Ikhlas (active c. 1586 – 1610), and only the figure of Akbar was painted by Madhu, a well-known 16th century portraitist.

The picture shows an event in the campaign against two rebels, Bahadur Khan Shaibani and the younger Ali Quli Khan Zaman Shaibani. To get from Agra to the insurgents' base at Jaunpur the Emperor's troops had to cross the Ganges in June 1567. The water was very high at the start of the rainy season and the crossing exceptionally dangerous. Nevertheless, the Mogul ruler took the risk, thereby demonstrating his outstanding courage and energy. The fortunate outcome of this enterprise was generally viewed as a sign of imminent victory against the rebels.

The miniature follows the text very precisely. The main part of the picture is taken up by the raging river with only a small strip in the background showing fertile land: the area close to the town of Sakit (in today's Uttar Pradesh) where these events took place. At the centre of this composition is Akbar riding on an elephant with outstretched arm, pointing the way to his followers. He is surrounded by a densely packed group of men and animals. Elephants are expressly mentioned in the text, where the Emperor is said to have selected 2,000 of these animals for crossing the Ganges. Horses and soldiers are also to be seen in the water. All these figures are depicted in animated movement, but the composition nevertheless seems absolutely stable and orderly as a result of its balanced disposition. The edges of the picture cut through this depiction so as to indicate the size of the army.

As the close orientation of the image to the text shows, representations in the *Akbarnama* were supposed to be as close to reality as possible. They were not painted to serve the observer's aesthetic pleasure; they were meant to document events described in the text as accurately as possible.

Akbar is shown in a drawing by Abd al-Samad (1540–1595), who was born at Tabriz in Persia and later worked there in the workshop of Sultan Tahmasp I (1524–1576). In 1549, under Humayun, he came to the court at Kabul where he was active for almost 50 years.

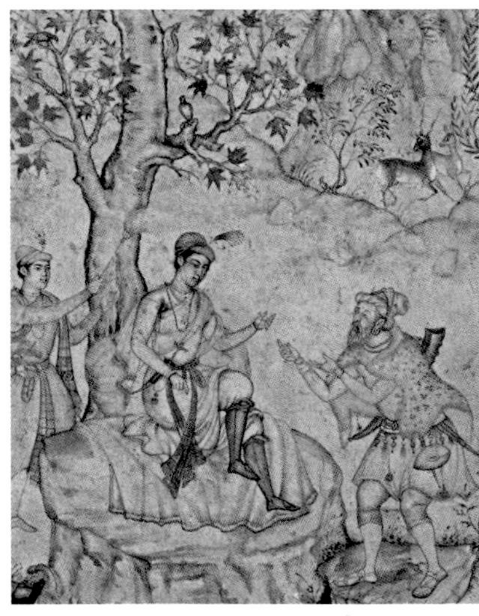

Abd al-Samad, Shah Akbar and a Dervish (detail), India, c. 1586

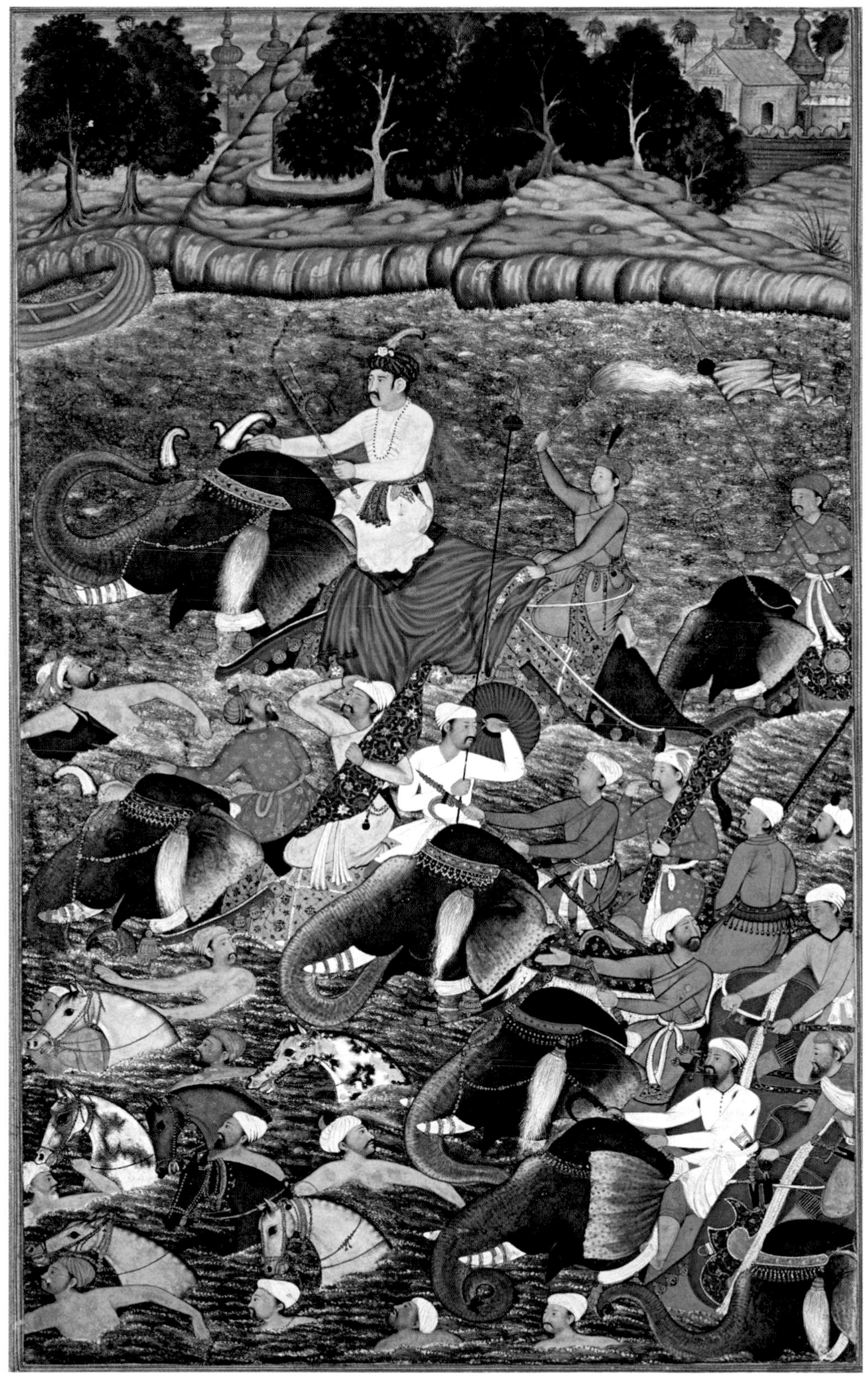

Prince Kurram is weighed in Gold, silver, and other Metals

North India, opaque watercolors, ink, and gold on paper, 26.6 x 20.5 cm
London, The British Museum

Weighing a Prince in gold was one of the Mogul court ceremonies marking the start of the solar year. This scene from a now lost manuscript with the memoirs of Mogul Emperor Jahangir (1605–1627) is set in front of the palace of Jahangir's son Kurram in Kabul's Urta Garden. Astrologers had cast a horoscope for the successor to the throne and prophesied success and wealth. Jahangir then decided that there should be a weighing in July 1607, celebrating Kurram's sixteenth birthday. Afterwards the coins and metal used for this were to be distributed to wise men and the poor in order to influence the Prince's fate positively through this act of benevolence.

In front of the palace is an entrance hall with slender pillars; inside this is a throne. In the building's wall are niches where Chinese blue-and-white Ming porcelain (1368–1644) is placed, imported at that time from India. A large vase is flanked by two porcelain women holding in their fingers little balls made from gems, stone, or precious wood. There are also objects of glass, rock crystal, and jade. For the weighing ceremony the ground is covered with costly carpets and an awning has been spread.

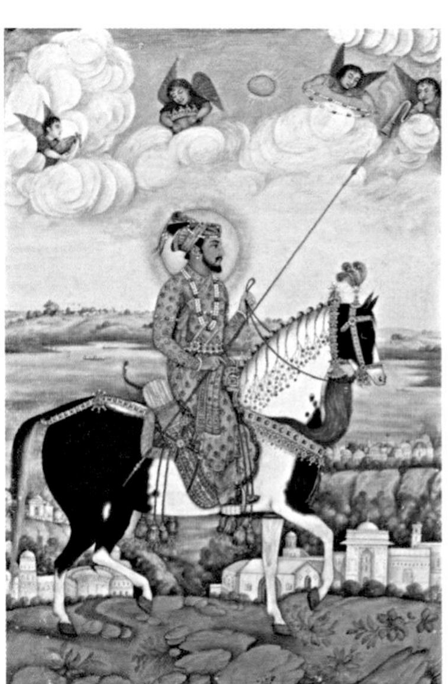

Equestrian Portrait of a Shah, India (Delhi), early 19th century

Prince Kurram (later Shah Jahan, 1628–1657) is sitting on a bed hanging from ropes, which is held by his father and a dervish. The seat is part of a bejeweled pair of wooden scales, and two officials are loading the other pan with little sacks of gold, silver, and other precious metals so as to balance the Prince's weight. On the right, next to the scales, are four important personages present for this occasion.

Jahangir, standing near the scales, is watching his son. He is wearing close-fitting trousers, an upper garment with a wide transparent coat, and a colorful belt. His turban is adorned with a bejeweled clasp. The centre of the carpet at the Emperor's feet is decorated with human figures: two women dancers and a tambour player.

In the foreground trays on the floor contain the Prince's presents for his father: precious textiles, esteemed since the Middle Ages as a means of payment and a special gift; knives encrusted with jewels, writing materials, and jeweled necklaces. A scribe is present to record these things for the inventory of artworks in Jahangir's collection.

This miniature is attributed to Manohar who must have done this painting after 1614 since Shah Jahangir is wearing pearl earrings. He adopted that custom after joining the moderate *Chishtiyya* dervish order in gratitude for recovery from a severe illness. Stylistic reasons suggest that the picture was done in 1618.

Comparison of this work with a 19th century picture of Shah Jahan on horseback makes clear how older traditions persisted in Mogul painting. An inscription wrongly attributes this depiction to Govardhan, a celebrated 17th century artist.

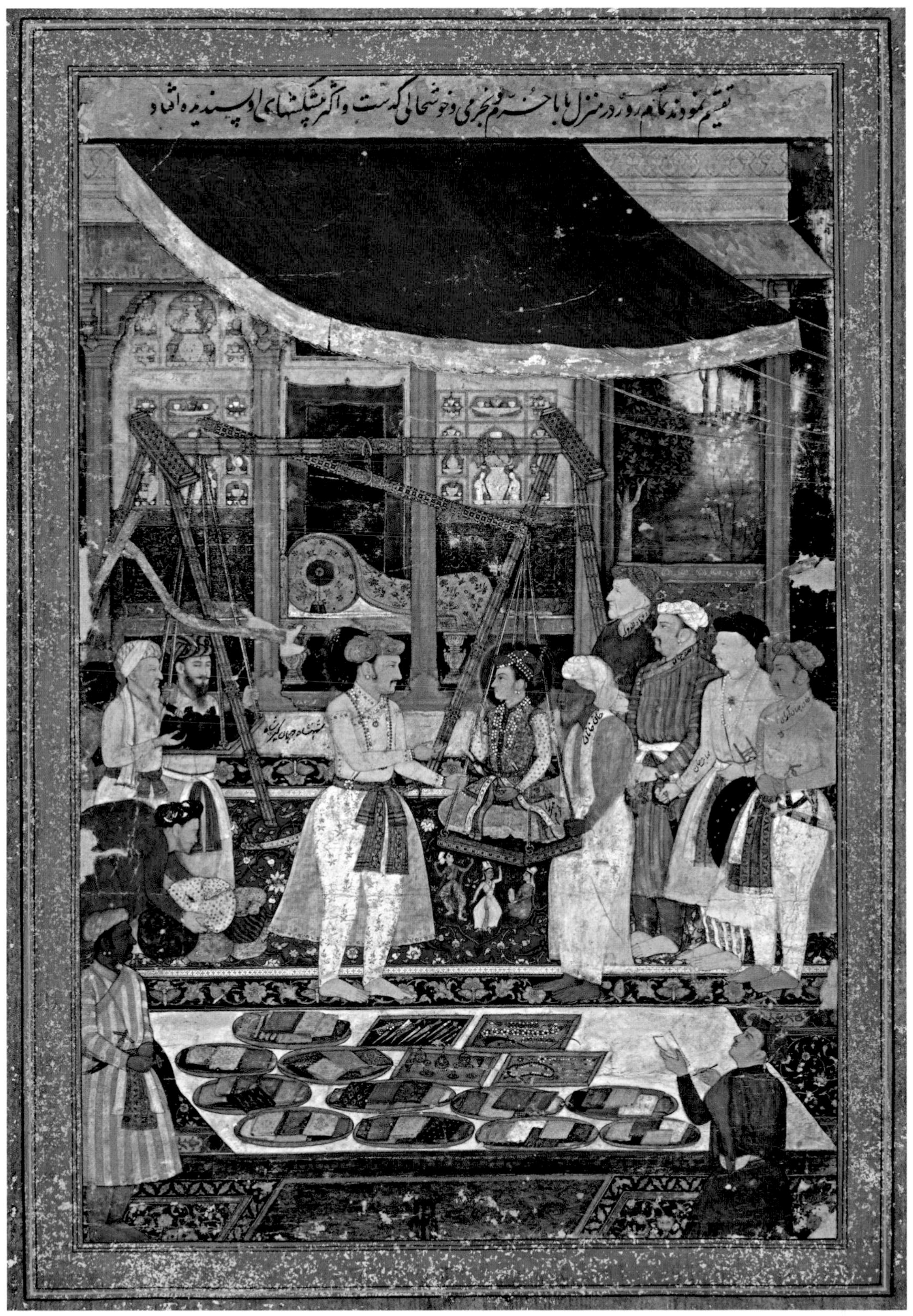

Rose-water sprinkler

Iran (probably Shiraz), *golâbdân* (persian), blown yellow-green glass, height 36 cm
Copenhagen, The David Collection

Rose-water sprinklers of colored glass were made in Persia from the 17th and 18th centuries onwards, particularly around Shiraz. Between 1638 and 1643 Jean-Baptiste Tavernier (1605–1689) became the first traveler to report the existence of three or four glass-producers in the city, making small containers for rose-water and perfume alongside bottles for Shiraz wine. Other Europeans, such as Jean Struys from Holland (in Persia 1672; d. 1694), also time and again mention glass production in Shiraz, as well as other travelers down to the 20th century. Vessels like the one shown here were chiefly made in the 19th century. They are notable for their special form, devised for pouring the precious aromatic oil. Out of a bulging body grows a long and irregularly wide neck, elegantly S-like in its spiral shape. This ends in a broad opening with a high, pointed lip from which individual drops of the perfume can flow. The bottles are made from colored (often blue) glass, which is frequently also decorated with additional colorful ornamentation. In 1930 glass-specialist C.J. Lamm wrote of rose-water sprinklers: "In the 19th century they became the vogue all over Europe because of their shape. Persian factories lost no opportunity for fulfilling this demand." These outlandish products were not just bought for private use; they were also frequently acquired for the collections of new Arts and Crafts museums where they could be studied by craftsmen and designers. American-born Louis Comfort Tiffany (1848–1933) was the first Western artist to create exotic vessels, the appearance of which was closely based on rose-water sprinklers. For him, oriental glass in general was a source of inspiration for the development of new materials and forms. Tiffany traveled to Egypt twice (1870 and 1908) to study ancient and Islamic glass there. He was above all fascinated by the iridescence engendered on the surface of glass which had lain in the earth for a long time. Stimulated by those models, the American glass-artist created an entire group of vases faithful to the form of 19th century rose-water sprinklers, but with multicolored shimmering surfaces based on what he had seen in Egypt. For that Tiffany developed a special process where the glass is covered with an iridescent surface. The impact of this material, which he called *Favrile* glass, is somewhere between metallically shimmering luster work and translucent glass.

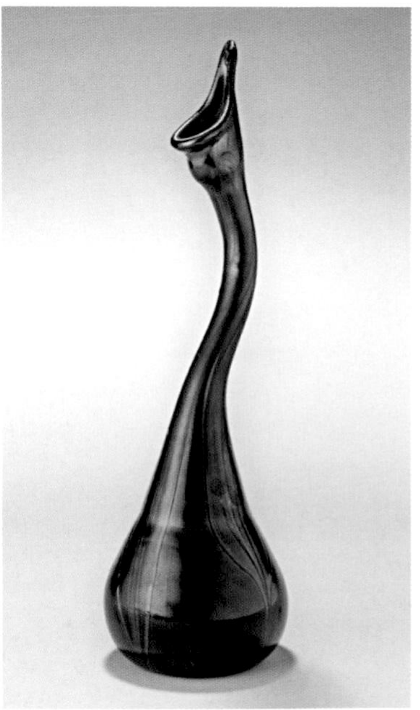

Louis Comfort Tiffany, Vase, c. 1896

Tiffany first presented his *Favrile* glass at the 1893 Chicago World Fair. His vases inspired by rose-water sprinklers and his new techniques were much admired everywhere in Europe and the USA around 1900, and imitated by glassfactories in France, Silesia, Thuringia, Austria, and Bohemia.

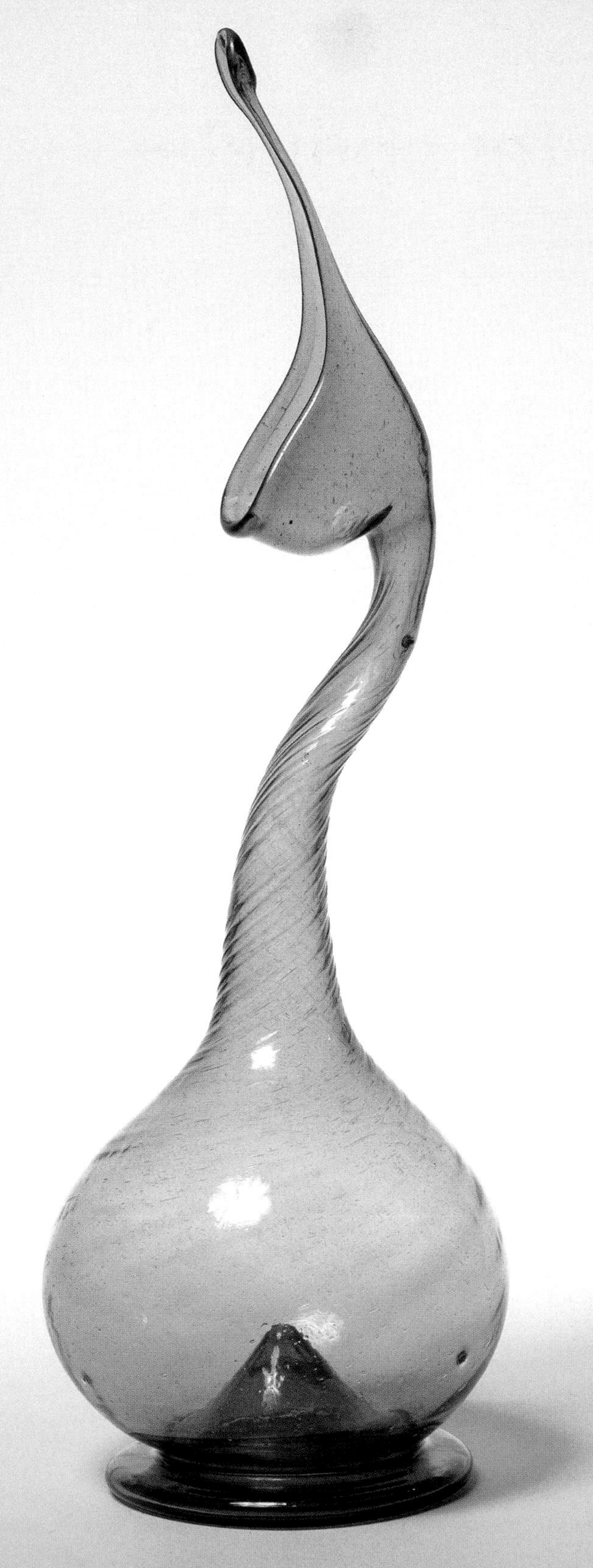

To stay informed about upcoming TASCHEN titles, please request our magazine at www.taschen.com/magazine or write to TASCHEN America, 6671 Sunset Boulevard, Suite 1508, USA–Los Angeles, CA 90028, contact-us@taschen.com, Fax: +1-323-463.4442. We will be happy to send you a free copy of our magazine which is filled with information about all of our books.

Hohenzollernring 53, D–50672 Köln
www.taschen.com

Project coordination: Ute Kieseyer, Cologne
Editing: Barbara Huttrop, Cologne
Translation from German: Tim Nevill
Production: Nadia Najm, Cologne
Design: Sense/Net, Andy Disl and Birgit Eichwede, Cologne

Printed in Germany
ISBN: 978-3-8228-5669-7

Copyrights:

The publisher wishes to thank the museums, private collections, archives, galleries and photographers who granted permission to reproduce works and gave support in the making of the book. In addition to the collections and museums named in the picture captions, we wish to credit the following:

Aga Khan Trust for Culture, Geneva: cover, p. 22, 23, 75, 90
The Art Institute of Chicago. Gift of Mrs. Charles F. Batchelder, 1974.524, photo © The Art Institute of Chicago: p. 76
Ayasofya Museum, Istanbul: p. 21
Bibliothèque nationale de France: arab. 5847, f. 121: p. 4; arab. 5847, f. 19: p. 37; suppl.turq. 190, f. 19: p. 63
© bpk / Museum für Islamische Kunst, SMB: p. 1; bpk / Museum für Islamische Kunst / Jürgen Liepe: p. 2; bpk / Museum für Islamische Kunst, SMB / Wolfgang Selbach: p. 7
bpk: p. 20, 31; bpk / SBB / Ruth Schacht: p. 55; bpk / Museum für Islamische Kunst, SMB / Andres Kilger: p. 81; bpk / Georg Niedermeiser: p. 34; bpk / Museum für Islamische Kunst, SMB / Jürgen Liepe: p. 42; bpk / Museum für Asiatische Kunst, SMB / Jürgen Liepe: p. 52
© The Bridgeman Art Library: p. 14 right
The British Library, © The British Library Board. All rights reserved, Or.6810, f.5v: p. 7; Add.18113, f.18v: p. 19; Add.7170, f.17v: p. 36; Or.6810, f.27v: p. 71; Or.2265, f.15v: p. 73;
The British Museum, © The Trustees of the British Museum. All rights reserved: p. 8, 79, 82, 93
© The Cleveland Museum of Art: Grace Rainey Rogers Fund, 1943.658: p. 18; John L. Severance Fund, 1956.10: p. 64; 2004. Purchase from the J. H. Wade Fund, 1945.169: p. 65
The David Collection, Copenhagen, No. 39/1967, photo © Pernille Klemp: p. 95
Edinburgh University Library, MS 20, f. 23v: p. 49
Gemeentemuseum, Den Haag: p. 83
Courtesy Israel Antiquities Authority: p. 16
Freer Gallery of Art, Smithsonian Institution, Washington, DC: Purchase, F1928.2: p. 11; Purchase, F1932.20: p. 12; Purchase, F1930.60: p. 28; Purchase, F1946.30: p. 35; Purchase, F1941.11: p. 47; Purchase, F1954.51: p. 51; Purchase, F1938.3: p. 59; Purchase, F1939.46a: p. 92
Harvard Art Museum, Arthur M. Sackler Museum, Alpheus Hyatt Purchasing Fund, 1952.7, photo: Imaging Department © President and Fellows of Harvard College: p. 21
Keramik-Museum, Mettlach: p. 84
LWL-Landesmuseum für Kunst und Kulturgeschichte Münster: p. 68
MAK – Österreichisches Museum für angewandte Kunst / Gegenwartskunst, photo © Gerald Zugmann / MAK: p. 87
The Metropolitan Museum of Art: Fletcher Fund, 1931. (31.119.1-2): p. 15; The Alice and Nasli Heeramaneck Collection, Gift of Alice Heeramaneck, 1980. (1980. 344): p. 46; Rogers Fund, 1918. (18.26.2): p. 53; Rogers Fund, 1924. (24.48.1): p. 89; all photos: The Metropolitan Museum of Art
Museum of Islamic Art, Doha, Qatar, Inv.No. MW.471.2007: p. 14
Nasser D. Khalili Collection of Islamic Art, London: MSS 727 f. 21a: p. 54
National Library and Archives of Egypt, Kairo: p. 41, 69
Courtesy National Library and Archives of the I. R. of Iran: p. 67
The National Museum of Fine Arts, Stockholm, NM K 76/1897, photo © Hans Thorwid: p. 94
Courtesy HRH Wijdan Al-Hashemi: p. 32

Reference illustrations:
p. 30: *Ewer*, Iran, 6th–7th century, beaten silver and gold-plating, decorated with three women dancers, 32.5 x 15.2 x 12.3 cm. Washington, DC, Arthur M. Sackler Gallery
p. 32: Wijdan, *Ala Allah*, 1993, oil on canvas, 50 x 45 cm. Collection of the artist
p. 34: Egyptian ceramicist, *Bowl*, Egypt (Fustat, Old Cairo), 11th–12th century, luster painting on ceramic, diameter 26.5 cm, height 5.8 cm. Berlin, Staatliche Museen zu Berlin – Stiftung Preussischer Kulturbesitz, Museum of Islamic Art
p. 36: Mubarak the Monk, *John the Baptist Receives his Name*, Iraq (Mar Mattai near Mosul), 1220, Syrian Jacobite Gospels, opaque watercolors and gold, miniature 22 x 25 cm, entire page 33.5 x 43.5 cm. London, The British Library
p. 40: Unknown craftsman in wood, *Minbar*, Egypt (Cairo), between 1468 and 1496, jacaranda, ivory inlays with 12-pointed star ornamentation, height 601 cm. London, Victoria and Albert Museum
p. 42: Muhammad ibn Sunqur al-Baghdadi (design), al-Hadj Yusuf ibn al-Ghawabi (damascening), *Qur'an Box*, Egypt (Cairo), c. 1320–1330, height 27 cm, breadth 42.5 cm. Berlin, Staatliche Museen zu Berlin – Stiftung Preussischer Kulturbesitz, Museum of Islamic Art
p. 44: *Box with Lid*, Spain (Medina al-Zahra), 966, ivory, silver hinges and lock with later engraved ornamentation, 10.2 x 20 x 12.5 cm. Paris, Musée des Arts Décoratifs
p. 46: *Medallion*, Iran, 11th century, diameter 17.1 cm, height 0.7 cm. New York, NY, The Metropolitan Museum of Art
p. 50: Johannes Itten, *The Archangel Israfil*, drawing in a diary, Germany (Berlin), 1926, entire page 29 x 22.8 cm (detail). Zürich, Itten Archive
p. 52: *Phoenix Among Flowers*, China, Northern Song dynasty, 10–12th century, silk, 33 x 30 cm. Berlin, Staatliche Museen zu Berlin – Stiftung Preussischer Kulturbesitz, Museum of Asiatic Art
p. 54: Unknown painter from Tabriz, *The Mountains of India*, Iran (Tabriz, Rashidiya District), 1314, opaque watercolors, ink, gold on paper, 29.1 x 43.6 cm (detail). London, Nasser D. Khalili Collection of Islamic Art
p. 64: Unknown Persian painter, *Festivity at a Princely Court*, Iran (Shiraz), c. 1444, opaque watercolors, gold and silver on paper, left-side of a double title-page, 32.7 x 22 cm. Cleveland, OH, The Cleveland Museum of Art, John L. Severance Fund 1956.10
p. 68: August Macke, *Merchant with Jugs*, Tunisia (Tunis), 1914, watercolor, 26.6 x 20.7 cm. Münster, Westphalian Museum of Art and Cultural History
p. 76: William Morris, *the "Hammersmith" Carpet from the hall of the John Glessner House*, Chicago, 1887, hand-knotted wool and cotton, 3.33 x 4.72 m. Chicago, IL, The Art Institute of Chicago, Gift of Mrs Charles Batchhelder, 1974.524
p. 82: *Plate*, Turkey (Iznik), c. 1550, quartz ceramic with glaze and painting in the Musli style, diameter 39 cm. London, The British Museum
p. 84: Villeroy & Boch, *Stoneware Plate*, décor no. 1404, Germany (Mettlach), c. 1885, polychrome decoration, diameter 55 cm. Mettlach, Ceramics Museum
p. 90: Abd al-Samad, *Shah Akbar and a Dervish*, India, c. 1586, opaque watercolors and ink on paper, miniature 23 x 16 cm, entire page 39 x 25.4 cm (detail). Geneva, Aga Khan Trust for Culture
p. 92: *Equestrian Portrait of a Shah*, India (Delhi), early 19th century, miniature, opaque watercolors and gold on paper, 26.8 x 18.1 cm (detail). Washington, DC, Freer Gallery of Art, Smithsonian Institution
p. 94: Louis Comfort Tiffany, *Vase in the form of a Persian Rose-Water Sprinkler*, c. 1896, height 36 cm. Stockholm, National Museum

Page 1
ANONYMOUS

Calligraphy in the form of a Hoopoe:
"In the Name of God the Merciful"
Iran, 17th century, pen and ink drawing
Berlin, Staatliche Museen zu Berlin – Stiftung Preussischer Kulturbesitz, Museum of Islamic Art

Page 2
ANONYMOUS

Simurgh and Zal
Iran, c. 1530–1540, Safavid miniature from a *Shahnama* for Shah Tahmasp, tempera colors, gold-leaf, soot ink
Berlin, Staatliche Museen zu Berlin – Stiftung Preussischer Kulturbesitz, Museum of Islamic Art

Page 4
Attrib. YAHYA IBN MAHMUD AL-WASITI

The Eastern Islands
Iraq (Baghdad or Mosul), 1237 (Abbasid), miniature from a *Maqamat* ("Assemblies") by Muhammad al-Hariri al-Basri (1053–1122), entire page 25.9 x 28 cm
Paris, Bibliothèque nationale de France